People, Common Sense, and the Small Business

Patricia Tway, Ph.D.

BETTERWAY PUBLICATIONS, INC.
WHITE HALL, VIRGINIA

Published by Betterway Publications, Inc.
P.O. Box 219
Crozet, VA 22932
(804) 823-5661

Cover design by Rick Britton
Typography by Designations

Laws pertaining to fair labor practices are constantly changing, and may even vary from state to state. For these reasons, the author recommends checking with local and state agencies for information pertaining to these practices.

Library of Congress Cataloging-in-Publication Data
Tway, Patricia
      People, common sense, and the small business/Patricia Tway
         p. cm.
      Includes index.
      ISBN 1-55870-245-8 (paperback) : $9.95
      1. Small business—Personnel management. I. Title.
HF5549.T89 1992   91-44682
658.3'03—dc20   CIP

Printed in the United States of America
098765432

This book is dedicated to all our employees.

Acknowledgments

I did not use names for all the companies or people in this book. I excluded some company names to avoid both name-dropping and unwanted publicity. I excluded some people's names because I wanted to focus attention on issues, not personalities. I also wanted to make it easier for the reader to glean messages from the material by not having to remember a series of names.

In my academic field work I often exclude names for a third reason, to protect those who do not wish to be identified. I had no problem with that in this book; in fact our employees wanted to be identified. To satisfy their wishes and mine I have excluded their names in the narrative but have included them with their letters.

Which brings me to the people I want to thank who have contributed in some way to this book or my work: Dr. Robert Secrist, my professor and academic mentor; Jean Zuckerman, my publicist and friend; Marilyn King for her wise counsel; Dr. Linda Tway, who critiqued the manuscript; and last but foremost my husband Gene, who made it all possible by giving me a big job to do and then letting me do it without interfering.

Foreword

The buzzword in business today is employee "empowerment." Pat Tway has been working this way for fourteen years. Visitors to the Tways' company always remark about three things: the enthusiastic people, the immaculate workplace, and the high quality product. Those are the ways you evaluate a company and rate a manager. She developed a very special work force, but then she is special.

I met Pat Tway with her husband, Gene, at a cocktail party, quite by accident. I say accident because I almost never go to business cocktail parties. But I did that night and I'm glad. Pat had recently designed the china for Jimmy Carter's flyfishing cottage. I was the interior designer for the cottage and was anxious to see the china that President and Mrs. Carter had created with Pat. I invited the Tways to my office and the next day they showed me the china. I was delighted with it.

As I talked with the Tways, I was impressed by Pat's natural enthusiasm. She was so excited about the Woodmere employees and what they could do, I found myself wanting to do business with them. I also found myself wanting Pat to be guest speaker for my lecture series. I asked her right then and she accepted.

For the past twenty-one years I have invited professionals from the business world to address students as speakers for my Spiegel Lecture Series at the Carleton Varney School of Art & Design, a college within the University of Charleston. My school is dedicated to helping students develop the technical skills, intellectual clarity, and professional attitudes necessary to become good designers. I have high standards and select speakers with high standards, who are knowledgeable in their fields and enthusiastic about their work. My speakers have broad work backgrounds and an interest in learning. Dr. Tway certainly has both.

Her background as a hard worker is impressive. What is more impressive is her attitude toward work and people. After she spoke at my school, my director, Jo Kerr, wrote, "I have rarely seen the students as excited as they were about Dr. Tway's visit. The students were so enthused we decided to have a ceramic design contest. Dr. Tway agreed Woodmere will produce the china and donate it to the school if you [Carleton Varney] will select the best design submitted by the students."

Imagine my surprise when Pat called after her visit to the school and said, "You have given me the best day and the worst day of my life." I asked how, and she said her best day was the day she spent as a Spiegel Lecturer. Her worst day was the day she read the newspaper's account of the event, which incorrectly credited her with one of my designs. Even though I tried to put her at ease, telling her I was used to misprints, she apologized profusely, called the newspaper, made them correct the mistake in the next publication, and sent it to me. She was insistent that they get it right. "Carleton Varney designed the Greenbrier Gold china service and Woodmere produced it."

She readily admits mistakes and wants others to do the same. That is one of her basic management techniques. She points out that knowledge is based on recognizing mistakes and believes poor quality is caused by workers ignoring mistakes. In her book, she tells you how to correct this attitude.

In recent months, Pat Tway and I have shared a design together, when we created the official Vice Presidential china for use in the Vice President's Residence in Washington, DC. Working with Marilyn Quayle, the design of the china, in soft blues and golds, complements the rose and blue decor our office planned for the main floor of the residence on the grounds of Washington's Naval Observatory. Pat's creative task was to interpret the styles of Mrs. Quayle, yours truly, and herself, in a china pattern—and I must say Pat did achieve this most admirably.

I like to work with people who share my standard of excellence, but there aren't many around in American industry today.

The quality of yesterday is hard to find. That is why it is so refreshing to read Pat's book. Her emphasis on positive attitudes is one of the keys to her success. Instead of complaining about Japanese competition and asking them to slow down, as some top CEO's have done, she has learned from them and used their production and quality as a challenge for her own employees, a challenge they relished and met. She shows how we can reclaim our place as a nation of quality workers who turn out quality products.

Her training techniques work, and when it comes to employee "empowerment" read Chapter 9. Her employees' letters say it all, and are an inspiration to anyone who works with people. They validate her common sense approach to management.

What you will enjoy most about Pat's book is her how-to approach, because she doesn't bore you with theories. She gets right to the point and shows you how to do it with examples that work.

Carleton Varney
President, Dorothy Draper & Company, Inc.
Dean, Carleton Varney School of Art & Design
University of Charleston

Contents

Dr. Tway's book, People, Common Sense, and the Small Business, *makes sense for any business.*

Dorothy Sarnoff, Chairman
Speech Dynamics, Inc.

Introduction

This book grew out of my own experiences as co-founder, co-owner, and co-operator of a small business. Our business grew from a "mom and pop" operation with ourselves and a college student to over a hundred workers. When we got that big we decided we weren't small anymore and pared down to half that size, where we were more comfortable. We wanted to stay small.

We started our business because my husband, Gene, was disillusioned working for corporations, and I was in a position to put to good use what I had learned from industrial research. I had earned a doctorate in anthropology, studying language and work in a china factory. Afterward, I continued my research and published a number of articles on such subjects as production flow, employee training, quality control, and management relations.

Our backgrounds prepared us for starting a small business. Years ago, we had both worked in direct sales, where individual effort is rewarded. We had both worked at some other jobs too. My past work history was a checkered one: professional vocalist, copy writer and women's editor for a radio station, fashion coordinator, designer and promotion writer in the jewelry industry, and sales promotion director for a cosmetic sales company.

Gene had been a musician, a shipyard worker, an accountant, and a salesman. He moved from sales to marketing to vice president and board director, as he climbed the corporate ladder. The higher he got, the more frustrated he got. While he had the satisfaction of seeing his marketing and sales ability develop business for others, he was not rewarded commensurate with his contribution or effort.

The marketing concepts he had learned on the job, the sales techniques he had developed over the years, and the self-confidence he had gained in direct sales were not being put to good use. And he was frustrated. When a corporate decision cut his bonus, wiped out the division he had built, and "promoted" him to another marketing job to develop another division, he'd had enough. I agreed.

Like a true entrepreneur, he decided we should start our own company. But what do you do for money? We used our small savings, borrowed a great deal, took a partner for a short time (we bought him out the first year), and Gene worked at three consulting jobs while developing our first accounts. What was I doing to help out?

Luckily, my doctoral studies and factory research were in the same industry in which he was establishing our company. I was still researching the china industry and teaching part-time at three universities. With that as background, I was ready to help out.

Our small business started as a marketing company in the china industry. We marketed several private label china patterns, which were produced for us. We added our own manufacturing facility when our suppliers could not keep pace with our growing sales. In our china decorating plant, we created designs, produced decals from those designs, and applied them, along with gold or platinum lines, to undecorated china purchased from suppliers in England and Japan. We also decorated china on a contract basis for other companies. (See Figure 24 on page 207 for a detailed description of our process.)

When we started our company, we took the approach that there is room for all of us in a growing, thriving industry. There still is. The problem is never the competition. The problem is how we respond to the competition; knowing what we want to do and being the best at it, then finding where we fit in an expanding, changing market created by the changing competition.

In anthropology we call this "finding your ecological niche." I'll use an analogy. Species survive, even thrive, over long periods of time based on their ability to exploit an ecological niche in the general environment. For example, a small lizard thrived in the same general environment as a huge dinosaur because it exploited a different ecological niche. So too, small companies like ours and yours can thrive in the same general industrial environment as giants, because they exploit different market niches.

With that approach, we decided to fill a need in the American marketplace. That's what you have to do: know where you have to be to fit the competition. Remember, if there is competition, there is a market. Once you have decided where you want to be, decide how you are going to get there. How are you slightly different or unique? What can you do that others aren't doing or won't do? Or what can you do better? You should know this before you invest your money in your business. Then get going, but be prepared to make sacrifices. We did.

When we started our business, we had, like most Americans, acquired a big mortgage on our home and a number of responsibilities to go along with it. We had a farm with four horses, four dogs, three cats, and a daughter in college. I mention her last because she was not home where she could help the family enterprise.

We had one college student living with us to take care of the animals. We gave her board and room and paid her the going rate for yard work to take care of our sprawling lawn, feed and care for the animals, and house sit when we had to travel. And we had to travel a lot to get the business started. At first, we couldn't afford for me to travel, too.

It's tough when you first start your business. There is never enough money, and you worry each day that it will be your last in business. A banker told us the life of your business is limited to how long you have been in business. If it's one day, then you can survive one more day. If it's five years, your company's life expectancy is five more years, etc. If that's true, then you really are living from hand to mouth when you start your own business.

I remember looking at the feed bill for the horses and knowing we couldn't afford it, but we couldn't part with them. We let them eat the grass from our lawn and the apples from the trees that grew near the barn. We cut corners a dozen other ways, just as you have if you have started your own business.

Our office started in the upstairs bedroom. Gene used a public secretarial service until we could afford to hire one. Later we hired a secretary. She had to come to our home each day to type letters and process sales orders. The college student and I shipped from our garage, and Gene sold big accounts using our home phone. I remember how proud we were when we got our first business telephone. Gene still remembers when he bought our first printing calculator and how worried he was that we had overspent. By the time we sold the business and had installed a computer system throughout our offices and factory, neither of us could remember what it cost.

For the first few years, I worked only part-time in the business and taught at several universities. After we added the manufacturing operation, we moved our business to a building we rented on the edge of town, and Gene hired a young manager. Within a year our business was in serious trouble. While our marketing end of the business was succeeding due to Gene's efforts, our manufacturing end of the business was failing due to the young manager's inadequacy.

Gene asked me to join the company full-time to reorganize and manage the manufacturing end of the business. It was an opportunity to apply what I had learned from my research at the china factory. I had learned what to do, but also what *not* to do when managing a plant. I agreed to come on board and began developing the methods and techniques described in the following pages.

Within four years we built our own 16,000 ft. building. Our financial situation improved as the business prospered. We were able to attend industry trade shows, and later, to take some of our employees to Hawaii and other places on business trips. Our business required us to travel frequently to the Orient, to England, and to other countries. Before we sold, we had grown from a small business to a multimillion dollar operation. Our product is in the homes of the Vice President of the United States, the King of Saudi Arabia, and a former President. We did all right.

The following pages won't tell you how to market your product. That's another book I need to write with Gene—because that was his expertise and his part of the business. Except for the design work I did for our company, we never crossed into each other's domain. His job was marketing, finances, and sales. My job was hiring, training, managing, and developing the people who worked for us.

Which brings me to an important point. If you have a partner, whether you are man and wife, relatives, friends, or business acquaintances, use the same approach. Stay in your own area of expertise. Don't play in each other's sand box. It's the only way a partnership in business can work successfully.

1.
How to Provide
a Good Workplace

Most of us have to work. In fact, we spend the major portion of each day working. It is only natural for people to want to work in a good place. Operating a small business is the best way to provide a good place to work.

It is only natural for problems to occur on the job. Often these problems aren't big ones, but any problem at work can be irritating and a source of unhappiness. Some relate to intangibles such as human relationships, while others relate to tangibles such as the physical environment. That's why it's important to have management policies that keep all problems, even minor ones, to a minimum —so everybody has a good place to work.

When we started our small business, there weren't any books that addressed our problems. That's why I used a common sense approach when I had to manage and develop people for our company. It worked for us. I believe it will work for other small businesses if you operate on two premises: (1) Each person will be at work each day in order to do the right thing. This is what I call having good attendance. (2) Each person at work wants to do the right thing. This is what I call having a good attitude.

With good attendance—being at work so you can share what you know and good attitude—approaching daily problems wanting to solve them—common sense can be used to make a good workplace.

Providing a good place to work is a prerequisite for having good people. Several things contribute to a good workplace. Here are some of the tangible and intangible features: (1) good value system, (2) individual focus, (3) open door attitude, (4) stated goals and policies, (5) adaptive behavior, and (6) good physical attributes.

VALUE SYSTEM

A *value system* provides the foundation for everything you do. Your approach to life is determined by your value system. When you define your value system, you have more control over it and its ramifications. Anything you bring to the level of awareness, you can control and change.

Pearl Buck wrote about the difficulty she and her children had adjusting to the American value system when they moved to this country from China. They had lived in China all their lives, where the value system taught that it was good and necessary for a person to report all mistakes, his or her own and others'. The Chinese value system taught it was a person's duty to help others know when they made mistakes. It was considered good and necessary because it helped improve society. A person who reported mistakes was considered a responsible, caring citizen.

Pearl Buck related that after coming to America her children repeatedly came home from school in tears because teachers had punished them for reporting mistakes. The teachers called them "little snitches" and "tale carriers" and told them they were bad children. The children didn't understand because they had been taught to report mistakes. It was part of their value system.

Pearl Buck complained that the American value system that teaches us not to report mistakes can lead to problems for society. The system implies that it is not necessary or good to report mistakes. This ultimately leads to hiding them.

Equating Quality with Responsibility

The system implies that we are not responsible for our neighbor's acts nor for improving the society. In fact, we punish people who "blow the whistle." This attitude affects the workplace, where workers feel no responsibility to report what goes on around them. It leads to workers deliberately ignoring mistakes to avoid reporting them.

As a result of this value system, it's very difficult to get workers to report mistakes, even their own. It makes it difficult to solve work-related problems and leads naturally to poor quality—a major problem in American industry today. Poor quality is the result of mistakes that cannot be corrected or prevented without the cooperation of workers.

Reporting Mistakes

Having a good attitude toward admitting and reporting mistakes is necessary if you want good quality. If employees are afraid to report mistakes because it might reflect on themselves, a company is doomed to poor quality. The way to solve the problem is to change this "no-responsibility," "no-fault" attitude—a formidable task for management. But it is not impossible. I know, because we did it in our small business.

Our company solved the problem by incorporating several management techniques at the beginning. We knew it was especially important for us to admit and report mistakes because our company wanted to be recognized for its high quality. We saw the need to change the attitude toward admitting and reporting mistakes if we were going to get the cooperation of workers to maintain a very high quality level. Mistakes would have to be seen as a natural part of the learning process. A worker who made a mistake would be corrected privately, not punished or ridiculed. A worker would be penalized only if the worker knew about a mistake and didn't report it. Consequently, workers felt more secure and were less likely to hide mistakes.

With this basic notion, we did several other things. We freely admitted our own mistakes. We let everyone know we considered mistakes accidents that needed correcting, not crimes that required punishing a person in public or denigrating him or her in private. We knew management sets the tone for employees. How you respond to mistakes affects how employees respond, and we wanted them to respond in a positive way.

We did other things to change the employees' response to admitting and reporting mistakes. We gave bonuses for reporting mistakes. If a worker from one department noticed a mistake in another department and reported it, she or he received a bonus. All bonuses were awarded at a general meeting. The worker who had made the mistake was not mentioned but corrected privately. Part of the process included complimenting that worker on other things done correctly and encouraging the person to do better.

By continuing this policy over the years, our company trained all workers to expect this procedure. Supervisors held meetings and included sessions in which they discussed their own mistakes and how they could have corrected them. Workers admitted their mistakes and looked on them as a natural part of learning and developing.

Your basic value system can have other ramifications for your business. For example, our value system included the notion that individuals are responsible for their acts and control what happens to them. How they think determines what they ultimately become. The Hindus teach: a thought becomes an act, an act becomes a habit, a habit develops a character, and a character reaps a destiny. How you think, so you act, so you become, and so things happen to you.

Since the individual was of utmost importance to us, we worked to provide an environment that was conducive to maintaining relations on an individual basis, not on a group basis. This was promoted by our backgrounds.

My husband, a salesman, was paid a commission based on his efforts. Later, he worked for large corporations that gave yearly pay raises and bonuses across the board. He worked harder and developed more business than others but got the same rewards.

As an anthropologist, I studied a china factory with a union in which workers were treated as groups. I worked closely with the union president and asked him what he considered would be the ideal work environment. To my surprise, he said a small company that deals with people like individuals—without a union.

When I asked why, he said if you deal on a one-to-one basis you get things settled faster, fairer, and easier. He said it's difficult for a third party to come in and know what's going on, and it takes too long. Some union grievances take three years to settle. A small business can settle them in a day.

This union president described other things for the ideal work environment: a good health plan, a good dental plan, pensions, insurance, vacation time, holiday time, adequate lunch and coffee breaks, and a clean place to work. We did what he suggested and added: sharing of knowledge, decisions, financial information, and profits.

We incorporated all those things in our small company. The extent to which we did was exemplified by a National Labor Relations Board representative, who commented that if all companies treated their employees the way we did, there would be no need for a union.

This, together with other commendations we received from our industry and others on a state and national level while we owned our business, testifies to the good work environment we provided. You can do it too. But you need to state your value system, your goals and policies, and be careful they are compatible. If they are not compatible or not implemented, it won't work.

We believed an ideal work environment would have to incorporate several things: a value system that was workable; a predictable environment so workers would feel secure and know they had control over what happened to them; an open door policy so individuals could communicate on a one-to-one basis with the president or the packer; a flexible viewpoint so individuals would know exceptions would be made when circumstances warranted it; a reliable demeanor so trust could develop and workers would know they could achieve what they wanted through their own efforts; policies that supported company goals; behavior that implied respect for others and their territory; and good physical surroundings.

You may have a different value system or another way of expressing what you want for your company and employees. Define it, and it will provide a foundation for all your goals and policies.

INDIVIDUAL FOCUS

Operate with individuals, not with groups. It's important to treat people as individuals. People who are treated as groups suffer from two things: lack of confidence in themselves as individuals with power to control their work; and lack of confidence in the company's ability to deal with them on an individual basis.

If you work with individuals on a one-to-one basis, those individuals don't feel they must get together as a group in order to be heard. They know that as individuals they have the right, responsibility, and power to solve their problems. Problems can be solved quickly and without disruption to other workers if second or third parties are not involved. We found it easier to operate on this basis.

Handling Unpleasant Situations

Operating on an individual basis puts a great responsibility on the employer to settle grievances rapidly, to get to the bottom of things, and to have the courage to face unpleasant situations. Unpleasant situations never go away. Many managers feel if they ignore something or don't correct a person, the problem will solve itself. This seldom occurs.

When you ignore confronting unpleasant situations on an individual basis, you subconsciously give up your responsibilities as a manager. In effect you're saying, "I told them what the rules were but I'm going to let them break them. I'm not going to keep the rules either. I told them I would let them know when they made a mistake or did something wrong, but I'm not going to let them know." That causes mistrust. Companies that foster that kind of mistrust deserve unions because the people in those companies need them for predictability and protection.

It's unfair to inform workers that you will tell them how they are doing and then not tell them. If you don't tell them, they can't learn. You can never correct something if you don't know it's wrong. This is poor management and invites a union.

Corporations that hire managers and then neglect or refuse to point out errors in behavior or work do a great disservice to the managers and to the company. Whether they do this out of a false sense of loyalty to "stand behind the managers you've chosen" or whether they just want to avoid a confrontation, the result is the same: poor management.

Operating on an individual basis also brings new responsibilities to the employees. In an autocratic, hierarchical work environment, the employees are not responsible for themselves as individuals but as members of a group. They are taken care of by others. Operating on an individual basis, they are expected to take care of themselves because they are responsible for themselves. If employees want to work in a predictable environment, each individual must keep company policies. One of those polices has to be an open door policy.

OPEN DOOR ATTITUDE

Be open in your relationship with employees. If you communicate with them on a one-to-one basis, you will have less difficulty in everything you do. You cannot have that kind of relationship if your management is hierarchical. Each employee must feel free to communicate with *anyone* in management. If you must have an organization chart, design one with connecting lines on the same level, rather than ladders or boxes on different levels. You can use a star, circle, or grid pattern.

I believe such a chart better illustrates the basic concept: that every worker in your company is valuable, but in different ways. As the founder of your company, you may have worked at every job. If your company has grown enough to hire workers, those workers know things about those jobs that you don't know now. That makes them uniquely valuable to you. Of course they can be replaced. So can you or anyone who works for your company.

The unique contribution of each person contributes to the total value of your company. If you lose sight of this, you lose sight of their individual worth and begin treating them as groups. When you do this, you are inviting a union. You may want to have one. If you grow to a very large size, you may need one. My experience indicates a small business can work successfully and more effectively without a union—if you do it right.

Let Employees Share Problems with You

When we owned our small business, every employee and every supervisor in our company knew she or he could come to my office and discuss anything. A month never went by that someone didn't come to me with a work-related or personal question. There has to be a feeling of mutual trust before this can occur. Workers have to feel secure, and they can only feel secure in a predictable environment.

Here is an example of a personal problem one of our new employees shared with us when she needed help. Her car burned up one morning on the way to work, so a towing service took it to the garage and told her it was not repairable. She was still making payments on her car to the finance company associated with the car agency where she bought it. Her husband had abandoned her and wouldn't pay child support, and she was afraid the finance company would demand payment. She couldn't make the payment if she couldn't work, and she couldn't work without a car.

I called the car agency and explained her dilemma to the top manager. He asked me what he should do. I suggested he take the car back and fix it or let her trade it in on another one. He could add the cost of the repair bill or the newer car to her current bill and extend the payments. I pointed out it was just common sense to help her. If they didn't help her, she would lose her job and go on welfare and food stamps and become a tax burden to him and everyone else. He agreed to help if the finance company would. I called and got their agreement, then called the towing service and explained the problem, and they agreed to tow her car to the agency for nothing.

I then called a quick meeting of supervisors to ask for their help. Someone suggested she call the legal service agency for help with her marital problem. One supervisor told her about a housing authority that would give her money toward her housing costs if she qualified. Another supervisor told her about a fuel allowance agency that would do the same thing.

While still in my office she called legal services. They told her how to file the necessary information through their office to obtain a legal document forcing her husband to pay child support and about the county Children's Services that would follow her husband to garnishee his wages if necessary.

By the end of the day her problems had been solved. I called the car agency, finance company, and towing service and thanked them for their help and sent them some porcelain as an added token of our gratitude. I told them they were the kind of people we liked to work with, and if we had anyone who was looking for a car or towing service we would send them over. Helping her took some time and effort, but we all felt it was worth it. Before we sold the company, she had become a supervisor's assistant.

Sharing the Company's Problems

An open policy with employees also implies sharing some of *your* problems with them. When you have decisions to make, invite them to participate. You'll find they will give you ideas, and you will see things a different way. You will also find that the ideas you give them will help *them* see things a different way. They will be more co-operative with you. They will know you respect them because you asked for their opinion, and they will respect you for asking their opinion. Mutual respect is the foundation of mutual trust.

An open door policy also means you share financial information with your employees, not in detailed accounting terms that confuse them, but in general terms they understand. Companies that share this knowledge with workers have an advantage over companies that don't. By letting workers know how things are going, you automatically let them know you have nothing to hide, you are "up-front" and "above-board." If companies never let workers know how things are going, they can never expect the workers to understand or sympathize with their problems. They run the risk that the workers suspect they are hiding something. Later, when large profits or losses are revealed, and somehow they always are, the workers may be resentful. Sharing financial information has some disadvantages, but the advantages far outweigh them.

Let's look at some disadvantages. Workers can become frightened and feel their jobs are not secure, especially if the current period statement isn't a good one. They may even wonder if they should be looking for another job. Most workers have never been permitted to share financial information. Many of them don't want to know. When companies share this information with them, they are being invited to share the bad with the good. Workers are accustomed to an autocratic environment in which they are taken care of and kept in the dark. Now they are treated as responsible individuals who have the right and the obligation to know what is happening. They are no longer in the dark, but the light you shed with your financial information may not be welcome, at least in the beginning.

The first time we shared this information with our employees was during a bad period. In addition, those workers had never been invited to share that kind of information. Most of them said, "Don't tell us these things. We don't want to know," or "Why are you upsetting us like this?" We said we considered them part of the company and wanted them to share the company's problems and solutions.

As part of the company, they had the right and the obligation to know what was happening. They had to know why the company couldn't give them bonuses. We felt if they knew about the problem and how it related to them and their work, they would be in a better position to understand. They would become part of the solution, looking for ways to help; rather than part of the problem, being resentful for not getting bigger bonuses.

We felt they would be aware of how crucial they were to helping solve problems. We wanted their ideas and suggestions for how we could do a better job, how we could save money and improve production and quality. They would now know the company was doing all it could to help and that we had nothing to hide.

The positive side of sharing information is typified by our workers' reactions as they became accustomed to sharing financial information. They all became more interested in how they were doing. Morale was high, motivation of workers was easier, and the attitude throughout the plant was changed to one of more understanding for the company and its problems.

If you haven't considered sharing financial information with your employees, start now, even if the picture looks grim. Maybe that's the best time to start. Workers will respect you, and they will have a positive attitude toward what they can do to help in the future. But this only works if you have an open door policy that invites communication.

STATED GOALS AND POLICIES

Your company's *goals and policies* determine other things you do. Your value system determines *how* you do it. Each company sets goals. Your major goals set your company in the direction you want to go. Your minor goals support the major ones and must be met in order for the larger ones to be satisfied.

Try to project a positive attitude toward the company goals so your employees will reflect that same attitude. Since goals are met through the efforts of employees, it's important for them to know what the major and minor goals are. It is of primary importance to hire the right people, on the right basis, and to give them the right training.

We preferred hiring people who had no work experience in our industry, because of the new techniques we were innovating in our decorating methods and the new management policies we were innovating in our company. We believed it would be easier if our people had no preconceived notions about what would or wouldn't work. An additional benefit of having no work experience is that these employees don't have sloppy or lazy work habits to break.

We tried to hire the best people we could and to obtain the finest products we could get. We purchased only the finest quality ceramic colors and handled them with care. We conducted experiments that required using tight controls. We used laboratory weights and measures, worked systematically, tested one variable at a time, and maintained accurate records.

If your goals include a high quality product, you need to be meticulous in everything you do, including your housekeeping. The walls, floors, and ceilings of areas where experiments are conducted have to be kept as clean as you can get them. The fuel you use may be determined by your company goals. Ours was. We used electricity because we had to maintain as clean an environment as we could.

We had our office and plant walls painted white, our office floors carpeted in light tan, and our plant floors painted light tan. The light colors provided an ideal work environment and forced us to maintain good housekeeping habits. We had to have our carpets vacuumed and our floors scrubbed each night, even in the warehouse. Our goal was to maintain laboratory conditions throughout the plant. Our daily quality control checklist for our office and manufacturing facilities was nine pages long.

Sometimes you will receive additional benefits from your major goals if you support them with the minor goals. For example, by maintaining an immaculate work environment and training our employees to be careful, we saved hundreds of dollars in maintenance insurance the first year—money with which we bought a special machine for one of our departments.

When the vendor saw how clean our facilities were and how careful our employees were, the cost of the first year's maintenance insurance was waived. Maintaining the ideal work environment can pay dividends with other insurance policies. If you have no major accidents and very few minor ones, you set a standard that implies great care.

We were especially careful to follow through with our management policies. We insisted on daily memos relating to all tasks—from phone calls to important quality control meetings. We found the higher the standard in minor duties, the more apt each person was to maintain those same quality standards during experiments because the habit of being careful was already established.

We set goals for departments to conduct a certain number of experiments each month. As a result, one department found a new way to use standard equipment that increased our productivity and income. Setting goals for each department fosters a general attitude of anticipation for new ideas and new ways of doing things. We awarded bonuses for new ideas. We found ideas were generated by keeping in touch with others in our industry, so we sent our people to industry seminars when we could.

Standard Policies

Our policies supported our major goals. We had a no smoking policy from the first day we started our company. We knew smoke would not be good for our work environment. We had a no eating on the job policy because we knew any food or beverage could contaminate the work environment. We had a policy requiring employees to wear safe shoes and clothes that would not embarrass us when important clients or vendors visited. We also had a policy regarding visitors.

Visitors Policy

When visitors come to your company, it's a good idea to have them register when they arrive and when they leave. Any number of reasons justify a visit by outsiders. They may come to take a tour, to apply for a job, to sell you something, to service a vending machine, to examine some portion of your shop in order to make a job quote, or they may "just need to look you over." Whatever the reason for the visit, have visitors formally register. It shows you are a quality company.

Some companies have a very tight policy regarding visitors. They may even require an ID button while visiting and not permit visitors to bring a camera. Other companies allow visitors to photograph different areas of their organization, but only with permission. Some companies have an employee accompany visitors everywhere they go. Other companies let visitors walk unaccompanied through certain sections of their office or shop.

Visitors policies may be strict or loose, but they are necessary, whether your company is large or small. I have visited large factories and small shops in a number of countries. The good ones have had a policy requiring visitors to register and to be accompanied through their facilities. It's as much for the convenience of the visitor as for the employees, who are trying to work. For example, one company I visited in Thailand neglected to have an employee accompany me through one section of their plant, and I got lost.

The size of your company and the work you are doing will dictate how strict a policy you need, but you do need some sort of policy to keep your company organized and running smoothly at the quality level you want.

When our company was first getting started, we made the mistake of letting clients, potential customers, salesmen, accountants, job applicants, plumbers, electricians, carpenters, and other people visit without formally and consistently signing in and signing out.

Consequently, we were never sure who was on the premises, or who had been, how long they had stayed, or even why they were there. Vendors dropped by whenever they were in town, seemingly without any objective except to take our staff's time. Service reps came and went at will. Even our CPA's assistant, who regularly visited our accounting department, didn't notify our office staff, so that often the president, who had wanted to ask him questions while he was there, was unable to do so. As a result, we wasted a lot of time, and we had difficulty maintaining the quality standards we had set for ourselves.

When we received the bills from some of the companies whose service representatives called on us, we thought the bills were considerably higher than they should have been. Some companies did not invoice us properly. Others itemized the charges on the invoices, which included parts, service calls, and labor hours, but the amount of time they listed for labor hours at our shop was not accurate. The hours were noticeably in excess of the time the repairmen had spent on the premises, but we couldn't prove it because we had no record of their visits.

When we checked with our supervisors in the shop to get their opinions, they told us that one service rep was not even on the premises at the time he listed it with his employer. Instead, he had only stopped by the plant and then had left immediately, to make an emergency call. The supervisors also complained that the service reps often wasted their time by visiting with them, rather than working on the repairs and then leaving.

At our next weekly supervisors' meeting, we discussed the problem and jointly decided to institute a policy that required every visitor to register when he or she arrived and left. This included anyone who visited the plant for any reason.

Here was the policy we instituted: each visitor had to register, listing his name and company, the person or department he was visiting, the reason for the visit, and the time of arrival. The person he was visiting was notified, and that person either accompanied the visitor to the appropriate department or, in the case of accountants and vendors, asked the visitor to go to the proper department where he also registered. After the visit, he signed out from the department he visited, listing the time, and signed out the same way in the front office before leaving.

If the visitor was a service rep making a repair call in the shop, the supervisor for that department was notified and came to the front office to accompany the visitor to the department where the visitor signed in. After the business was completed, the visitor signed out with the supervisor, then proceeded to the front office and signed out again.

I called our CPA, the vendors, and the service companies and told them about our new visitors policy, asking for their cooperation. After we instituted the policy, we noticed three things: a more careful itemization of charges by service companies, a reduction in our service bills, and a more business-like approach by the service reps when they visited the departments in our shop. There was no more idle small talk with supervisors. The service people came, did their work, and left. Their work improved in quality, and so did ours.

One owner of a service company called to tell us that he appreciated what we were doing because he discovered several of his service reps had been padding their hours, stating that they were at our company longer than they had been. He said that our new policy was improving his company's quality and saving him money because he was able to keep closer track of his employees in the field.

It's just common sense to have a policy requiring all visitors to register when they come to your company. It will save you and your employees time, and it will save your company money. It will also show visitors and their companies that you operate in an organized, business-like manner even though you are small.

Your goals and your policies, even your visitors policy, set your standard. Try to provide the best you can. We put a copy of the following statements in the employee manual and the company handbook.

Organization Policy

Our company was organized based on the suggestions of a wise man who said that a good company that recognizes individuals, provides a clean, safe work environment, has good benefits and pays good wages based on individual ability and effort doesn't need a union. The man who said this to me was the president of the Steelworker's Union at a pottery. We took his suggestions.

For fourteen years our company has successfully operated with these principles, in addition to providing a profit sharing program. At our company YOU (the individual):

Control how fast you grow in your job.

Control how much you earn.

Can try other jobs when available.

Are promoted based on ability regardless of how new you are.

Are rewarded and recognized for your length of employment.

Receive bonuses based on effort and attitude.

Receive bonuses for helping report quality problems.

Receive bonuses for making suggestions to improve us.

Have your questions answered immediately.

Have your problems solved privately and quickly.

Have the freedom to work without paying dues or fees.

Have the freedom to speak for yourself.

ADAPTIVE BEHAVIOR

Proper behavior and respect for an individual's work space contribute to a good workplace. Sometimes what you *don't* do is as important as what you do at work. If you stop to analyze the behavior of people you try to avoid on the job or people workers don't like, you will probably notice they have similar habits—sitting on people's desks, sitting on tables, putting their feet on furniture, or slouching. This behavior implies an attitude that is too casual for work, or it gives the impression that they don't care about the situation. It may imply a takeover attitude or a lack of respect.

Taking someone else's chair or place at a business meeting, unless you're asked to do so, is another bit of behavior that is taboo. We generally associate status with certain territory or objects. People are creatures of habit, and even if you are not assigned a regular place in a conference room or dining area, chances are you habitually sit in the same area. If someone else takes that spot, you unconsciously resent it. If that person continues to occupy your space, you will tend to have an aversion to them.

How you sit in a chair can affect the way people perceive you at work. For example, a man who walks into a conference room, grabs a chair, turns it around backwards, and spreads his legs apart to straddle it while leaning forward over the back of the chair creates a negative effect, especially with women employees. This behavior signals locker room camaraderie and doesn't belong in the workplace. Even for a small company it is too casual.

Sitting behind someone else's desk or in his or her chair without permission is another behavior pattern that automatically signals you're taking over and may create resentment in your coworkers. Showing disrespect for someone else's workplace or objects they use is another behavior pattern that is taboo.

Even assuming control of a workplace too soon can create a bad image. For example, one man who was hired to replace the retiring president of a small company sat in the president's chair before being formally asked to do so by the president. In addition, whenever the president was gone from the office during the transition period, the new president sat on the president's desk, put his feet on the desk, and used personal items the president had left on the desk. Other people resented this and mentioned it to the office manager. This was a behavior pattern he might better have avoided if he wanted to make a good initial impression with the people he would soon be managing.

He had other behavior patterns that created a negative effect: coming in late, leaving early, and frequently taking days off. When someone mentioned the importance of management keeping all the rules to set a good example, this same individual said, "What I do is nobody's business." The other retiring executive tried to point out that in a small company what anybody does at work is everybody's business because, "We all share in the company's profits and losses." Within a year or two this bad manager had to be replaced.

To be certain your behavior won't affect you adversely at work, study the behavior of others. Try to notice what others do that bothers you. You may have similar habits that bother other people.

GOOD PHYSICAL ATTRIBUTES

Physical attributes play an important part in providing a good place to work. If people feel good about what they see, they feel good about you and your company. This applies to your customers, your vendors, your reps, your investors, and most important, your employees. If all these people are proud to be associated with you and your company, they will give you bigger orders, better service, more sales, another loan, and increased loyalty.

Furnishings

Try to provide the very best place to work. At first, you won't have enough money to buy new office furniture, storage cabinets, shelving, production tables, or other necessary fixtures, but you can still have an attractive workplace that will look like new. We did. Here's how.

Start with used furniture and fixtures. My husband's first desk in the spare bedroom was a flush door supported by two metal file cabinets I bought for fifty cents apiece. When he got a used metal desk, he felt richer than he did when he ultimately bought an oversized walnut conference desk for his last office.

You can make good buys from ads, private individuals, used office supply stores, and regular office stores. Ask them about damaged goods they can't return, or special order items customers didn't take, or overruns, or slightly used items they have on consignment.

Establish a good relationship with several new and used office supply firms. The more they know about your needs, the more apt they are to call you or be on the lookout for items for you. Keep in touch with them. We called three good suppliers regularly.

Distributors and manufacturers of shelves and fixtures are another source for things you need. We bought used steel shelving from a firm several different times. I told the salesman to let us know anytime they were stuck with an overrun. He called one day and had enough shelving to double the space in our warehouse. A company had ordered the new shelving and went out of business before he could deliver it. The trick to supplying your company with all you require is never to stop looking.

We got our tow motors and other machinery the same way. We started with used equipment and moved up to new. When you buy used machinery, be careful and check the warranty and the contract before you sign. When the machine is delivered, refuse to sign off until you know it works. When we first started our business, our warehouseman signed off on a machine and it didn't work. It cost us several hundred dollars in attorney's fees to get out of the contract. It was clearly my mistake, and I made sure the warehouseman knew it.

Always paint and repair the used items so they look like new. There are companies that electronically paint anything metal and make it look like new. If the desk tops or table tops are damaged, have new Formica ones installed. This isn't expensive, and it is worth the effort. Your goal should be to make everything look as if it were brand new.

The Look of the Workplace

Use mirrors on the walls where you can. They double the space visually and provide another source of light. Mirrors are not expensive, so have a reputable firm install mirrors six feet high or higher across walls behind desks and in spaces that are dark or appear cramped.

Paintings and prints add color and interest to a workplace. We used a number of them throughout our offices and the plant. We used huge Marimekko prints in the plant to make it as attractive as the front offices. Select the wall hangings to add interest but not distract workers. Keep personal items such as plants, calendars, and family photos to a minimum. Your place will look less cluttered. Keep all sexy pictures out of the workplace. Decide how you want to look, then set the example.

One of the lessons I learned from my factory research at the china plant was to provide offices for supervisors that were light, centrally located, and visually open. Each office had three sides of clear glass or Plexiglass. Every supervisor had a desk, chair, double file drawer, telephone, calculator, and any other items that made the job easier. Always think about yourself in any job when you are providing the work space or the supplies that will be used in that job. Ask yourself how you would feel working there.

Lunch Room and Grounds

You need a lunch room for employees. We did not want vending machines because we didn't want any outsiders coming regularly to our place. It is a good way for union organizers to look your place over. Instead, we provided coffee and tea, a microwave oven, and a refrigerator.

Employees brought their lunches or went to restaurants or stores nearby for food and extra beverages. Most of them used the refrigerator we provided and ate lunch either in the lunch room or outside on the picnic table provided.

You may not have the space to provide a picnic table or places to sit outside. But you should make sure the outside of your building and the surrounding grounds are attractive. If you have a lawn, keep it mowed. If you have shrubs that need trimming, trim them. You may want one of your employees to take care of the grounds. We did.

If you use workers for more than one job, make sure you schedule their time consistently so they can manage two different jobs. Otherwise, one job or the other will suffer because of the divided time. One of our warehousemen cut the grass, but his job in the warehouse was so important to us that we couldn't use him to plow the drive in the winter. That was our busiest season. Therefore, we used an independent contractor for that job.

You will want to assign someone the job of keeping the front walk swept in summer and salted in winter. If you make sure one employee does this first thing in the morning, your place will always look good for visitors. Train the worker to pick up any debris the trash man or visitors may have dropped. Make a checklist and train the worker to use it. (See Figure 1.)

If you have a no-smoking policy and workers must go outside to smoke, provide a large, attractive sand-based ash tray. You will also need to enforce a policy requiring every smoker to discard cigarette butts in the ash tray, not on the grounds or near their cars.

Your major goal should be to provide the very best working conditions you can. If people like where they work and feel good while they are there, they will automatically like to come to work. You work there too, and you should want the best for yourself to enjoy your job. Most of us spend more time at work than anyplace else except home during any twenty-four hour period.

Figure 1
MAINTENANCE CHECKLIST

Item	Date Done
1. Check oil in truck	_____
2. Change oil in air compressor	_____
3. Drain water from compressor	_____
4. Drain water from shrink pack machine	_____
5. Check tow motor battery for water	_____
6. Oil cart wheels	_____
7. Check grease fittings on kiln wheels	_____
8. Clean tape machines, oil cutter bars	_____
9. Check band saw motor	_____
10. Check furnace filters	_____
11. Change oil on decal cutter	_____
12. Put two motors on weekend charge	_____
13. Check light bulbs	_____
14. Clean rain gutters	_____
15. Check air pressure in truck tires	_____
16. Oil all plant doors	_____
17. Lubricate pump with auto chassis grease	_____
18. Grease 3 roll machine	_____

JOBS THAT NEED TO BE DONE

1. _____
2. _____
3. _____
4. _____

2.
How to Find the Right People

When your business grows beyond what you can handle personally, you will face the problem of finding and employing others. Most small businesses that grow beyond the single entrepreneur often employ family members first, because it's cheaper and more convenient. Whether family members are a part of your original staff or join your labor force later, it's a good idea to establish and maintain a businesslike relationship with them during working hours. If you can't do this, don't hire them. Even if family members join your staff, your business will probably grow beyond what you and your family can do, and you will need to hire additional people. There are several ways to find employees.

Finding the right people for your small business is a never-ending job. But you will find your job is easier if you use several different sources: (1) employment agencies, (2) ads, (3) referrals, (4) temporary help agencies, (5) independent contractors, and (6) service companies.

EMPLOYMENT AGENCIES

Employment agencies offer a rich source of applicants. There are several kinds of employment agencies. Many companies use a state or federal employment agency. If you decide to use this source, make a personal visit if you can. If not, call and establish a working relationship with one or two people. This will give you the advantage of having a person who is acquainted with your needs and knows the type of person you want. It saves you time, so you don't have to describe your company each time you call. Ask as many questions as you can about their requirements, the tests they give, and what they expect of you as an employer.

Private Agencies

The other type of employment agency that is very effective — especially if your company requires people with a broader background and special skills—is the private employment agency. This type of agency requires a fee either from the applicant or from the employer. The fees vary with each agency and with each type of job.

Agencies we used in our area required 10% of the applicant's first-year starting salary for our particular jobs. We found applicants were more successful when they paid this fee. They had a vested interest in succeeding and therefore tried harder. It is important to clarify at the beginning who is to pay the fee. This will prevent misunderstandings and avoid unemployment claims.

When you call the private agency, give as much information as you can about your business and the type of person you seek. Invite the person you speak with to visit your company if he or she can. Don't be intimidated if your company building is small or is a building attached to your home or located nearby. Remember, you represent a source of income for the private employment agency. You are the buyer—they are the seller. They are selling you their services.

Get a copy of the contracts the agency uses for applicants and for employers and have the agency representative describe their services in detail. You want to know how reputable they are, what they expect of the applicant and your company, and what the applicant and you can expect from them. Unlike government employment agencies, a private agency will probably assign a person to handle your account. If they don't, ask the name of the person who helps you and try to get that same person each time you call.

Reporting to the Agency

When working with any employment agency—government or private—be courteous and helpful by reporting back when they send you applicants. When you don't like the applicants they send, try to be specific about what it was you didn't like. What skills did they lack? Was it their attitude or their general demeanor that was wrong for your business?

Rather than criticize the employment agency for sending the wrong person, find something to praise. Maybe they responded quickly; maybe they sent several applicants to please you. It's a good idea to assume some of the responsibility by saying, "Hi, this is (your name) from (your company name). I want to thank you for sending the applicants as fast as you did. We really appreciate it. We weren't able to hire them. They weren't quite right for us." At this point tell why and be specific. Then say, "Perhaps it's partly my fault for not giving you a better description of the type of person we need." Then try to point out the attributes you *are* looking for in applicants.

If employment agencies continue to send you applicants that are not right for your business, stop calling them. It is a waste of time to work with people who don't understand what you want. Instead, cultivate those agencies that do send you the best people and respond to your needs by working your account promptly.

Don't be discouraged if some agencies are not eager to send you a large number of applicants. We discovered one of the agencies we used was hesitant to send us many applicants for secretarial jobs because they thought our starting salaries for those jobs were low. They wanted to make a larger fee; consequently, they sent more applicants to other employers who offered higher starting salaries. We felt we were right so we did not raise starting salaries for those jobs to satisfy the agency. Instead, we explained in detail how we differed from other companies. We told them our policy was to hire at a lower salary because within a short period the secretaries would be getting more money than the other companies paid for the same amount of employment time. We preferred to give frequent pay raises as individuals acquired new skills. We did not give automatic yearly pay raises as the only incentive. We gave pay raises as frequently as the individuals earned them.

As the agencies became better acquainted with us and we could show them records to support our statements regarding our frequent pay raises, they sent us more applicants. We continued working with them and hired a number of the people they sent us over the years.

In addition to being courteous and helpful, be sure to communicate with the agency and the applicant when you have hired someone they have sent. Tell them the starting salary and give them any other information they need, such as the starting date and the duration of the probationary period.

Your Responsibility as the Employer

When you talk with the applicants, be sure you tell them you communicated with the agency. Repeat what the agency has told you about their agreement terms. Sometimes people don't understand what agencies tell them. And sometimes agencies forget to tell people what they should. Your responsibility as the employer is to make certain you are not involved in a misunderstanding between the agency and the applicants during the interviewing and hiring process. This will prevent problems and avoid unemployment claims.

If, after you hire the applicants, the agency calls to tell you the employees are not making their fee payments, tell the employees about the phone call. You may want to have a conference call with the employment agency, the employees, yourself, and another manager, as a witness. Or you may want to notify the employees in writing and tell the agency to handle it themselves.

We took a personal interest in our employees and tried to help them solve problems that related in some way to their jobs. We did not withhold money for them to pay the fee for the employment agency. We felt that was stepping outside the bounds of the employer. You should counsel and advise but not meddle. There is a fine line you need to walk.

Once you establish rapport with several employment agencies, you can usually rely on them. Whenever you need more people, call them and describe the job you have open. Set a target date for interviews. If you are in a hurry, tell them, then call them at least every other day until they send you someone. Report back on each applicant and once again, be courteous, so they will be eager to help you by sending more applicants.

Campus Placement Services

Before leaving the subject of employment agencies, I want to mention another source of recruits—the campus placement service. While these are not employment agencies, they function in a similar manner. We used one for a short period when we needed sales service people for the office.

I visited the campus and worked with the director, who set up a series of interviews for me. I gave them the job specifications and information about our company, including the employees' manual and company handbook. They sent me a number of applications students had filled out for the placement service.

We carefully screened the candidates from their applications and set up interviews in the placement office. After interviewing candidates there, we invited them to visit the company and followed the normal hiring procedures, which included our applications, tests, and interviews.

Some college campuses allow you to conduct on-campus recruiting. They set aside special days for companies to come in and talk with students. We never used that source but you may want to try it. Contact your local college or university and ask for information pertaining to their on-campus recruiting policies.

ADS
Ads can be another source for applicants. You can use trade journals, small newsletters, or local newspapers. When we first started our business, we used only three days of advertising in a classified ad section of a popular newspaper from a nearby city. We had so many applicants, we were able to hire all the people we needed from that one ad.

If there is a high unemployment rate in your area, as there was in ours, you will receive so many replies you may not be able to process them. We weren't able to process all the applicants adequately, so we didn't use that source again until there was an employment crunch several years later.

If you use ads, decide what it is you want from the ad. Write it yourself as if you were the person reading the ad. What would attract you? Be very specific about the jobs you have available. Be aware of government regulations regarding the kind of ad you can place. The journal or newspaper you call will guide you.

If you use trade journals, be aware that they only appear monthly, and if you are in a hurry, you may not have time to use that source. If you use the small newsletters, you may find that the same time lag hurts your recruiting.

We had the best luck advertising in several neighboring small-town newspapers. If you use that source, you may want to advertise in the want ad section and in another section. For example, if you are looking for a manager or an accountant, you may want to advertise in the want ad section and the business section.

Using a "blind" ad means you do not identify your company. We used that type because we were in a heavily unionized area, and we didn't want to alert the unions every time we were hiring. Use your own judgment about identifying your company in the ad.

Answering Phone Inquiries

Specify in your ad the best time for applicants to call and who the applicants should ask for when they call. Make certain that person is trained to use the telephone properly in order to qualify the applicants and set up appointments for interviews. This will save you a great deal of time. But be careful. Companies spend thousands of dollars each year advertising for employees and waste almost as much money by not properly training their personnel to answer the phone. If the people answering the phone do not say the right thing, they will lose the prospective applicant before he or she can be interviewed. Or the applicants will come in with the wrong attitude.

To ensure your company doesn't make this mistake, decide what you want the person to say. Then write the script. But ask yourself some questions first. Do you want to say what the job pays over the phone? How much do you want to know about the person before setting up the appointment? How much time does each appointment need? When is the best time for you and your staff to conduct interviews?

After you have made all these decisions and know what you want from the ad, write down what you want to say to get people to come for an interview. Read it over, then memorize it so you can get the caller you want to come in for an interview on your terms.

If you are going to delegate that duty to other people, explain it to them. Tell them what you want from each caller and why. Then rehearse your script with them. Listen to them read it as you pretend to answer the ad. Do this with them several times until you are satisfied. Make sure they are doing it in a natural manner before you leave them with the task.

We found it helpful to train more than one person to handle the calls. Several people can answer the phone using the name you listed in the ad. It's best to make up a name; then everyone is aware of what the calls are about and anyone who is trained can handle the calls. Another reason for doing this is the convenience of using a different name for each ad so if you advertise for more than one job, which we did later on, you will automatically know which job the person is calling about.

To handle phone calls properly, you might want to use a short script like the one we used. When an applicant called we said, "(Company name), may I help you?" The applicant replied, "I'm calling about the ad in the paper. Is Pat Smith there?" We answered, "Yes, I'll call her," or "Yes, this is Pat Smith. Who is this?" The person would tell us and we would ask, "How do you spell your name?" then, "Where do you live?"

If the applicant objects to giving an address explain, "We are located in (give your address), and we need to know how near you are to work." She will usually tell you. Ask her, "Are you working now?" "What do you do?" Don't ask where she works. You really don't care at this point, and she may be reluctant to tell you.

Continue by giving information about your company: "Let me tell you something about us." After you give a very brief description of your company and the job(s) you have available, ask her if it sounds like something she would like. If she says no, thank her for calling, and ask if she knows anyone who would like that kind of job. If she does, ask her to tell the person about your ad. You may get an applicant this way. We did on several occasions.

If a caller says she doesn't know whether she would like the job but would like you to spend more time describing it, don't do it. Thank her for calling, but tell her you don't have time to go into more detail over the phone. If she is interested, she will come for an interview. Proceed with, "We are setting up appointments for the following time periods." Then give specific times and a choice of two time slots. If she is hesitant, either about liking the sound of the job, or about the appointment, thank her and hang up. The important thing with applicants—especially from ads—is to avoid coaxing them to come for an interview. People should want to work—you shouldn't have to talk them into it. If you do, you will regret it.

If ad applicants are not willing to give you any information about themselves, they are really not interested in working or perhaps they are too fearful. We found (the hard way) that if they don't give you any information about themselves on the phone, they don't work out as employees.

After your staff has successfully set up interviews and the applicants from that particular ad have been interviewed, have a review session with your staff and critique one another to see what each of you learned and how your script or your method could be improved.

You will get more people to interview from ads than from other sources. But you may find this costly for several reasons: the percentage of qualified applicants is not high; you need qualified personnel to handle the ad replies by phone; you need an adequate office staff to help applicants fill out forms and take tests; and finally, you need qualified people whose judgment you trust to help you interview the large number of people who will come for interviews. Probably the most costly factor is the amount of time it will take you and your staff to process applicants who come from ads.

To know whether or not your ads pay off, keep accurate records. There are several things you need to know: which newspaper elicited the most replies; which one resulted in the most interviews for particular jobs; and which one got you the most or the best employees. Then calculate all that in relation to your cost. Use the newspapers that give you the best overall results.

REFERRALS

Referrals from people you know or from employees are a good source for applicants. The best way to use the referral method is to call people or tell employees whose judgment you trust that you have a job opening. Tell them about the job and that you will be interviewing within the next few days. Ask if they know someone who might like to apply for it. If they can't think of anyone at that moment, ask them to think about it and let you know as soon as possible.

Be sure to give your referral source the same kind of information you would give the employment agencies, so he has an idea of what type of people you are seeking for particular jobs. Let him know he is not responsible for the success or failure of any person he recommends. If you don't make this clear in the beginning, existing employees may be so fearful about their responsibility that they will not send you anyone. Or they may be hurt each time you have a problem or terminate someone they recommend.

Employees are the best and most reliable source for new people and are most eager to recommend someone shortly after they have completed their training with you. They may recommend a member of the family or a neighbor. Since they work for you and they know what you expect from their own experience, they are usually successful at finding the right person. In a small business, sometimes it's good to have networks of families and friends. It can provide a friendly atmosphere and help to make everyone feel they are an important part of the company.

Hiring Close Friends and Relatives

There is a down side to hiring families and friends of employees. Close friends and relatives are expected to back each other in disagreements, which means personal loyalty may conflict with company loyalty. This can put a strain on their relationship with the company.

Think twice before you hire very close friends or family groups. Close, intimate alliances imply supporting one another as a group even when one of the group's behavior is questionable. That's what families and friends are for. If you are emphasizing the importance of individuals—not groups—you are treading on dangerous ground to hire groups or cliques for your organization.

We had mixed results in our company. At different times we had sisters working for us. In more than one instance, if one quit the other quit soon after. In one case, there was rancor because we let one sister go and the other felt obligated to quit. We had a supervisor whose husband's brother applied for work. We hired him and discovered we had made a mistake. The supervisor agreed we should fire her brother-in-law. Two days later she came and said her husband and mother-in-law were forcing her to quit. She was in tears and didn't want to leave her job. But she did. This is an extreme case and (thank heavens) a rare one.

Romance in the Workplace

You can also have problems with friendships at work, especially romantic ones. When we first started our business, we had problems with a warehouseman and a decal inventory clerk who fell in love. We tried repeatedly to explain the importance of maintaining a business attitude at work.

When our attempts to help them control their behavior didn't work, we finally had to make a decision about which one to keep. We explained our dilemma to both of them and why we were keeping her. She had no behavior, attendance, or attitude problems with us except for their romantic affair. He had a series of discipline problems on his employee record, and he was not as productive as she. They understood our choice and we didn't lose her. She eventually became a valuable sales service person in our office.

Another romantic friendship didn't turn out as well. Two supervisors became romantically involved. The woman did the pursuing after being warned repeatedly that it was interfering with both her work and his. The man swore he didn't care for her and would control his behavior at work. Within a short period she quit. He swore he wouldn't quit because his job meant more to him than she did. The following Monday he handed in his resignation.

Other Problems

On the other hand, we had workers and supervisors support the company over misguided friends and relatives. Several workers asked us not to hire applicants they saw during the interview tour because they knew the applicants would expect the employees to support them over the company if they caused trouble.

One supervisor agreed we should fire her brother after he became a problem. Each time we disciplined him, he told a different story to his sister. She was privy to the discipline measures but still had a tendency to believe him until she caught him lying about us. She came to us, apologized for having believed him earlier, and told us to fire him. We did. She remained with the company and eventually was promoted to night superintendent, assistant plant manager, plant manager, and vice president.

Whatever you decide to do about hiring friends and relatives, state it as a policy. If you have a company policy that prohibits hiring close friends or relatives, you need to explain why. Most companies hesitate to hire close friends or relatives because of the misunderstandings I have just described. The major point is to let your employees know what your policies are regarding recruits before they send them in.

Reporting Back to Employees

If you are going to use the referral method to get names, be sure to report back to employees when you interview their applicants. If you did not hire their applicants, it's best to explain why—in a nice way. We said: "We try to hire the person whose qualifications most nearly fit the job we have available. We feel this recruit isn't quite right for the job we are trying to fill at this time. We appreciate your effort to help us. Maybe your next recruit will be right for us."

If you decide to tell them more, select the most obvious and least controversial reason when you report back to your referral source. Here's an example.

One of our employees recommended a neighbor. Our interview team unanimously decided not to hire her for several reasons, one of which was her lack of transportation at the time of the interview. When we reported our decision to the employee who sent her, we gave lack of transportation as the reason. Then we added, "Maybe your next recruit will be right for us."

If you have trouble later with employees' recruits you have hired, be sure to maintain good communication with the employees who recruited them. If you sense any change in their behavior or attitude toward the company, explore it immediately; make certain they have all the facts regarding your decisions and actions.

Bonuses for Referrals

Some companies use monetary rewards for referrals, but we never did. One problem is the responsibility the recruiter feels. Another problem is the tendency for the recruiter to give you too many names, without giving enough thought to the person's qualifications. In addition, offering money for referrals can cause hard feelings with others in your labor force.

Finally, it's difficult to know when to pay for recruits, since their success with your company has to exist beyond the probationary period. If you decide to pay a bonus for referrals, establish a program first. It should include what you'll pay, when you'll pay it, and under what circumstances you'll pay.

Thank the Recruiters

Whether you pay a bonus or not, thank the recruiters. Let them know you appreciate their efforts and reward them with recognition either in a company newsletter or when you make company announcements.

Once again, if you use employee recruiters they should know they are not responsible for the success or failure of their recruits. Applicants are hired based on their own merits. The employees' recommendations will get them the interview—not the job. Nor will their "connections" save the recruits' jobs if the recruits don't perform adequately or if they create problems.

It's a good idea periodically to tell those few employees you use for referrals to continue thinking of people who might like to apply for work. You can never have too many applications on file. Using the referral method brings responsibilities, but it can be worth it if you are careful how you use it.

People Off the Street

What about people who come to your company off the street and apply for work? We always asked them why they came in or who sent them to us. If they were hesitant or said they didn't remember, we didn't interview them. We told them if they were truly interested they could go to the state or private employment agency and apply through them. We never hired an applicant who came off the street. Our instincts proved right. Later we learned that two different people who came to our company off the street were union organizers.

TEMPORARY HELP

Temporary help agencies will supply you with workers on a short-term or long-term basis. Some temporary help agencies supply only office help; others supply workers for unskilled, semi-skilled, and skilled positions. Today there are agencies that provide managers, inventory control specialists, accountants, clerks, mechanics, screen printers, artists, and photographers. Almost any position you might need filled can be furnished by a temporary help agency. There are some advantages and disadvantages to using temporary help agencies. Here are some advantages.

Advantages

Using a temporary help agency saves you money in advertising and time in interviewing and hiring employees. The agency has already sorted out the bad apples. Normally, an agency tries to match a person with an employer. You give the agency your job requirements, and they select one or two candidates for you to chose from or they may send someone immediately at your request. The person they send to you has had experience, adapts quickly, and doesn't require as much training as a new person.

A temporary help agency saves you the hassle of paying personnel costs such as worker's compensation, unemployment benefits, hospitalization, and insurance. The employee works for the agency—not you. Therefore, the agency is responsible for those costs.

A temporary help agency saves you the headache of dismissing unsatisfactory workers. Discipline and termination are their problem —not yours. Your agreement is with the agency—not with the employee. If you are dissatisfied, you request a different person next time. They do the rest.

Using temporary help from an agency gives you the freedom to have extra people during peak periods or for emergencies without hiring them permanently. If you decide to hire the person later, most agencies have a policy that permits you to do this.

That is another advantage to using this method—the opportunity to hire the temporary workers later. This gives you a chance to work with them before you make a long-term commitment. Most agencies will accommodate a client who wants to hire one of their people. Usually you must agree to use their services for six months, and then if all parties are agreeable you may hire that person.

Our company used temporary help for a short period and had a good experience. We eventually hired the two secretaries the agency sent. After the temporary people had been working with us for six months, I told the manager of the agency I was interested in hiring both women. The director asked for six weeks' notice to help them defray costs.

One secretary eventually became our executive secretary. The other secretary began working in the inventory control department. Both women were still with the company five years later when we sold it.

Disadvantages

There are some disadvantages to using temporary help agencies. The person you want may not be available when you want him or her. Temporary help are also sent to other companies, and the other companies may have priority over yours or may be willing to pay more.

The person you want may not be willing to work the schedule you require. Many people work for temporary help agencies because they only want to work part-time or for a limited time during the year. Or they may be working for the agency because they like changing jobs frequently. Also, the job you need filled may be too highly skilled or require too much training to make it worthwhile from a production or quality standpoint.

Another disadvantage to using a temporary help agency is the cost. The cost may be too high for the quality of worker you are getting. There is a need to examine carefully your particular job requirements in the context of the worker who will be sent to you. Remember, the money you save by not having to provide regular employee benefits to a temporary help person is eventually paid by you as a normal cost for using the agency. The agency has to pay the worker, cover costs, and make a small profit. The hourly fee you pay the agency may be from 50 to 80% higher than what you normally pay employees.

One way to assess the value of such a source is to have your accountant compute the cost of the wages you normally pay for the job plus all employee benefits, including insurance, health, dental, unemployment, and worker's compensation costs. If you find you pay close to what the agency is asking, you may be wise to use the agency.

Another drawback is the salary the temporary workers make. An agency charges you enough per hour to pay their workers and make something for themselves, so the people are working for lower wages than you are paying your own employees for that job. Also, they may feel like outsiders if your other employees are close. You need to find out how your employees will react to using temporary help and how you will orient them.

So why do it? Because you can easily stop using the workers at any time, as opposed to having the worry of laying off or terminating employees to halt those same costs. And you can call them back easily whenever you need them, as opposed to worrying about former employees who have found other jobs.

Before you decide to use workers from a temporary help agency, ask yourself some questions about your own organization and about the temporary help agency.

Questions to Ask Yourself

1. Which jobs do you have available that could be staffed by a temporary help person?
2. How much training is required before a person can perform the job adequately? Is it worth the extra cost?
3. How much experience is required to perform that job to your satisfaction? Even a semi-skilled job that requires little training may require a great deal of experience. That is, a job may be relatively easy to learn but difficult to perform rapidly without a good deal of practice.
4. How tight are your quality standards? Are they time consuming to learn or difficult to maintain?
5. When do you need additional people? During peak periods only? Do you need them periodically throughout the year?
6. Do you already have a source for part-time help, such as high schools, trade schools, or colleges? Are there independent agents in your area who could work for you when you need them?
7. Most important, how will your current employees view your decision to use a temporary help agency for additional people? How will you tell them about it?
8. How will you orient the temporary help who come to your company?

If you decide you need to use a temporary help agency, you need to ask some questions about the agency.

Questions to Ask the Agency

1. Does the agency have a policy covering damage their person might do to your property?
2. What kind of insurance coverage do they have for any injury the person might incur while working for you?
3. How much notice do you have to give them if a person they send is not satisfactory? Can you send the person back immediately without paying the full day's fee?
4. How much information will they give you about the person they are sending?
5. If the employee is clearly not up to your standards, does the agency have an exchange or refund policy to cover your cost and inconvenience?
6. Does the agency work regularly with businesses like yours with references you can call?
7. Can they verify how much training and experience their person has had with your kind of work?

If all these questions are answered to your satisfaction, you may find using workers from a temporary help agency is what you want to do. You may want to use them when you first start your business and periodically when you need additional help for a short time. It can fill the gap for short periods and give you additional employees without worrying about a long-term commitment.

It's not a good idea to rely on temporary help agencies as a primary source for employees because it may cause hard feelings with your permanent employees. Nor is it a good idea to use the temporary help agency as a primary source for finding applicants to hire on a permanent basis. That might cause hard feelings with the agency. They will soon discover you are using them as an employment base and not as a temporary help source. If they had wanted to be in the employment business, they would have done that instead of establishing a temporary help agency.

INDEPENDENT CONTRACTOR

The *independent contractor* is another source for help when you need it. We used this source for our cleaning services and for odd jobs such as carpentry work. We found it cost us no more than having the same work done by employees and saved us some headaches. In some cases, it was cheaper because we didn't have to pay overtime. We used independent contractors for janitorial services. They came in daily at the close of the last work shift. We were satisfied because we were able to make them maintain our quality standards.

Using this method also automatically provides you with people who will do heavier cleaning for you, such as shampooing carpets and furniture. We found this system best because our company was small. When we tried to use our employees to clean, they were busy with other jobs. If we hired new employees as cleaners, we didn't have enough work to keep them busy cleaning full-time. Therefore, they had to be trained to work at other jobs. We began to rely on their production with those other jobs, and when we were very busy, we found it inconvenient to have those employees stop what they were doing in order to clean—which was their primary job. Consequently, we found it cheaper and more convenient to use an outside source.

Get a copy of the independent contractor's agreement and study it before you sign it. If there are things you don't understand or don't like, discuss this with the person. Satisfy yourself before you agree to use the service.

Generally, independent contractors are responsible for their own employee benefits, health insurance, and unemployment taxes. You are not responsible for anything except paying them on time. Remember, they are selling you a service, and it's important for you to be satisfied with it. When you aren't, let them know. Periodically, we had to remind our cleaning service people to improve their work, or we had to point out something they forgot to do.

SERVICE COMPANIES

Service companies will send workers to take care of your electrical or plumbing repairs or to haul away your trash. You will want to shop around to find people whose services and costs best fit your company's needs and your budget. When you find the ones you like best, use them. If you later discover they are no longer right for you, shop around and replace them. Just because they are not employed by you is no reason to settle for poor quality workmanship. Make certain workers from service companies understand the level of quality you expect.

When the service people arrive, have them sign in with their name, the date, the time, and the reason for their visit. When they leave, have them sign out. This documentation prevents misunderstandings about hours and wages. You'll find the service companies will appreciate your thoroughness since you are helping them keep track of their employees. We routinely sent these daily time sheets to our service companies.

Shortly after we started our company we complained to the service company that supplied plumbers. We felt they had charged us too much for the labor hours they worked. We showed them the signed sheets and learned one of their laborers was telling them he spent more hours on our job than he had. Our bill was adjusted.

LOOKING FOR THE RIGHT PEOPLE

As long as you are in business, you will need to continue your search for the right people. People move, die, or retire from the labor market, leaving employers with the perennial challenge of finding new employees. You will probably need to use each of the sources we discussed: employment agencies, ads, referrals, temporary help agencies, independent contractors, and service companies.

How often you use them will depend on how fast your business grows and how many people you need. If you use them effectively you will have plenty of help because you will have plenty of applicants. You will need them.

Rate of Return for Hiring

Your rate of return for hiring versus the number of applicants you receive from the various sources is determined by several things. The area in which your business is located has a great deal to do with it. For example, our company was located in a depressed steel region where jobs were scarce but a belligerent union attitude was prevalent. Repeatedly people answering the ads would flippantly say they would rather stay on unemployment, welfare, and food stamps than work for less than they had made at the steel mills. When we told what our jobs were paying, all the former steel workers would refuse to come for an interview.

On the other hand, we were in a rural area and the newspapers circulated in rural regions where people had a strong work ethic and were eager to enter the job market—women especially. With a rural location and a depressed area, you will find a number of people who want to work.

Other factors determining your rate of return include the caliber of people who apply and your qualifications, together with how selective you are. We were so selective that we stipulated in our ads and with the referral sources and agencies that we wanted applicants to bring evidence of their work in some handicraft—sewing, cake decorating, woodworking, painting, or anything that showed some interest and ability with hand-eye coordination. We accepted photographs as evidence of their work if they had given away or sold what they had made. We wanted people who enjoyed working with their hands and with colorful things—people who took pride in their work. Some of my most cherished memories are those I shared with applicants who shyly opened brown paper bags or boxes to show me what they had made. With the slightest encouragement or compliment, they would beam with pride and begin to talk about their favorite hobbies.

I still have several mementos I bought from applicants who offered to give them to me when I complimented them. I insisted on paying them for their work. Some of the applicants we hired, some of them we didn't. But I enjoyed sharing their handicrafts with all of them.

Stipulating these requirements severely limited the numbers of applicants we got, but it paid great dividends. We raised the status of the jobs in the eyes of the applicants, we gave them pride in their abilities, and we made them eager to work for a company that recognized their individual worth.

We did another thing that raised the status of the jobs in their eyes. We referred to our manufacturing plant as a decorating studio because in our region "plants" had a negative connotation as a "factory" and "a dirty place to work." If you find using a certain name or title makes a better impression and better defines what you do and what you are, then use it. It will improve the quality of people you get and may improve your rate of return for applicants who become employees.

If you look at our rate of return for applicants hired strictly from a numbers standpoint it doesn't look good: 100 applicants for 10 hired for 5 successfully trained for 2 key people. But if you look at it from the standpoint of the quality people we got and the enjoyment we had from working with them, it far outweighs the overall cost and extra effort.

Your rate of return is partly determined by the skill required to do your work and partly by your quality standards. We felt our entry-level jobs required at least three months' training. Our other jobs required six months. The highly skilled jobs (which represented the majority of jobs in our company) required a year of training and practice before the employee was performing to the standard we needed to make a good profit from his or her efforts. If your company does not require highly skilled labor, your rate of return for trained people versus applicants will be much higher.

Give a great deal of thought to the caliber of person you want and the effort you are willing to make to get that person. You will be in a better position to utilize the various recruiting sources that will help you find the right person.

3.
How to Hire
the Right People

There is no magic ingredient that can help you quickly and easily select a perfect employee. You may have already discovered not everyone wants to work, even though they go through the motions of coming to your business and filling out applications. Separating the "wheat from the chaff" can be an exasperating, perennial problem. But it is one you have to solve if you are going to stay in business.

If you successfully used one or more of the recruiting methods discussed in Chapter 2, you have several people to choose from. Your job is to learn as much as you can about the applicants so you can make the right decision.

If your company is a small business, you're lucky. You need fewer people, so you can be more selective and you can have a personal hand in selecting the right people.

Hiring the right people for your small business is a difficult job but not impossible. You will be successful if you carefully use the following tools and procedures: (1) applications, (2) tests, (3) company handbooks, (4) interviews, (5) calling former employers, and (6) deciding with caution.

APPLICATIONS

Applications are necessary, and you need to select the one that best accommodates your company's requirements. There are many stock applications available. Just be sure the one you select is government-approved so you are not asking something on the application that indicates marital, racial, religious, ethnic, age, or gender bias. It's a good idea to have your attorney check the forms you use.

Your application should include a statement that you are an

Equal Opportunity Employer. In addition, above the applicant's signature line, be sure there is a statement that the application does not create a contract of employment and that the applicant may voluntarily leave or be terminated at any time for any reason. That is for your protection and theirs.

A good place to inquire about the type of application you want is at one of the recruiting sources. You may not want to use the same ones they use, but they can tell you where to find different types. Our company used various application forms over the years.

The application form should give you some basic facts about people beyond name, address, and phone number. It should give you information about previous employment. Their work history may be important to you. Be sure to get all the information you can about their former employers, who supervised them, what they did, how they performed, how many promotions and pay raises they received. The more information you get on the application form, the better chance you have of uncovering something that might help you select—or reject—a particular applicant.

You may feel it violates your rights as an employer to be limited in what you can ask applicants. If you examine some of the questions you cannot ask, you will discover they are not important to you anyway. Do you really care whether a worker is married, black, white, or brown? Are all people of any religion automatically poor workers? Does ethnic affiliation limit a person's ambition?

Does age make a difference in ability to do the job? Before you answer, think for a moment. I said age—not physical condition. I have known some forty-, fifty-, and sixty-year-old people who were more active and energetic than some people half their age. Recent studies have shown, contrary to what was commonly believed, new employees in their fifties make excellent workers. They learn as fast, tend to be more cooperative, and take fewer days off than younger employees.

Does a person's sex make a difference for a job? It shouldn't unless there is so much strength required *no* woman could qualify. In that case, no small man could either.

In our business, I had to visit factories throughout the world. I saw men and women performing the same tasks. In one factory, women would occupy a particular job and men a different one. In another factory, the roles would be reversed for those same jobs. With today's tow motors and mechanical equipment, there is hardly a job small people, including women, can't perform. Gender does not determine what a person can do. Whether a person does fine, detailed work or solves abstract problems, gender shouldn't matter. Either sex can work successfully in most jobs.

Filing Applications

No matter how selective you are, you will have far more applications on file than you will use. What do you do with them? The government requires you to keep them for a period of time. Check how long the requirement is for your area and your industry. In the case of advertising, we set a time limit for accepting applications. If we used one of the other recruiting sources, we let our needs determine the time limit. At different periods, we were constantly processing one or two applications.

You need to have a system for classifying applications, so the ones you are still considering are available, and the ones you know you don't want are not in the way. We developed a system of classifying applications by primary and secondary job types and other details important to our company. We marked them one of three ways indicating whether we wanted the person, didn't want the person, or weren't sure. Ones we knew we didn't want because their qualifications did not meet the basic requirements for the job we put in the inactive file. Ones we knew we wanted and ones we weren't sure about we put in the active file.

Keep active and inactive files in separate places. As applications begin to accumulate, periodically box, label, and store the inactive applications for easy access in case the government needs to check them. Routinely review the active applications so you don't forget who they are. I made descriptive notes for myself and paper-clipped them to each application.

Sometimes applicants apply for one job but are better suited to another. Either their qualifications aren't right or they decide they don't want the original job. Yet they have other talents you think you might use in the future. Those are the applications you want to keep for future reference. You can notify the applicants later to apply again when you have other jobs available. You can't have too many good applications.

You *can* have too many résumés on file. With the number of instruction books and professional résumé writers today, there is hardly a résumé you can trust to reveal anything useful about the applicant. We found résumés to be filled with generalities and exaggerations. When you get résumés, examine the education, work history, career goals, and hobbies as you would on any application. Even with a good, well-written résumé rely more on your applications and tests than on résumés. We did.

TESTS

Tests are another tool you can use to select the right people for your business. There are a number of psychological and aptitude tests to help determine whether a worker would enjoy certain types of jobs, could perform certain tasks with ease, or has leadership qualities. There are also tests for clerical, secretarial, and accounting jobs. You may decide to use some of these tests to help qualify applicants. If you do, I suggest you also create some tests of your own that pertain to your company. We relied more on our company tests than on tests we could buy.

We bought and used stock tests when we were seeking employees with more technical training and experience. Since we developed our own managers, we administered these tests to all employees who were interested in learning more. If the applicants exhibited particular attributes during the interview, we often asked them if they wanted to take additional tests for future reference. If they did, we let them and put the tests with their applications.

If you are hiring artists, you need to see evidence of their work. Most professional artists have portfolios of their work. Even if they are in art school or just graduating, they have examples of what they can do. We always told the artists to bring a portfolio or samples of their work.

When you evaluate their work, be honest and keep it on a professional level not a subjective one. Limit your criticism and praise and be specific when you discuss examples that do or do not relate to your company's needs. You walk a fine line when you evaluate an artist's work.

Use Tests that Best Fit the Job

For most positions, we relied on tests we created that pertained to specific jobs in our business. If you are going to create your own tests, include tasks that are most important for particular jobs. Use the actual materials workers use on the job, and use the same tests for every person applying for that job. That way you are certain the tests are fair and accurate. It gives you a better tool for comparison, especially when you have to reject applicants.

The closer your tests simulate normal working conditions, the better the tests will be and the more likely you are to discover whether a person can or cannot do the job. If you use the tests properly and fairly, they can help you select the best person for the job and reject the others in a way that protects you from charges of unfair hiring practices. The object of tests is to indicate whose qualifications best fit the position you have available.

We relied on our own company tests for every position in our company, even though we might have augmented them with standardized tests for certain positions when necessary, such as those in the accounting department. You might want to do that, too.

For example, if applicants are interested in a secretarial position, have them take a typing test for accuracy and speed using an actual letter and envelope your secretary has had to type. Use company invoices to have them total the amounts with a calculator. They should take a quick inventory of a few office supplies, tally the inventory sheet, and demonstrate to you that they understand how to make entries and exits. When they are finished, have them proofread their work as a final test.

If they are applying for a warehouse position, give tests that indicate their ability to calculate how much space is needed for the items they will be working with. Use an actual problem your warehouse person has to solve as part of the warehouse test. The warehouse test we gave applicants was the same test we gave our employees who wanted to apply for a job in the warehouse. (See Figure 2.)

You might have them make entries and exits from warehouse, office, or other department inventory sheets you use. Test them on anything you think will help show what they can do or learn to do.

Figure 2
WAREHOUSE TEST

Date _____ Name _____

1. If there are 300 individual shippers in a bundle and 50 bundles in the warehouse, how many individual shippers are there? _____

2. If we use 3000 individual shippers a day, how many days will the 50 bundles last? _____

3. If there are 48 plates to a box and there are 45 boxes to a skid, how many plates are on a skid? _____

4. If a skid is 4' x 4', how many skids can be stored in a room 20' x 20' if they are stored 2 levels high? _____

5. How many plates can be stored in a 20' x 20' space based on this information? _____

USE THE BOTTOM OF THIS SHEET
FOR YOUR CALCULATIONS

Administering Tests

Applicants should be given enough time to take tests, but you need to set a time limit based on your experience. If your business is so new you don't have experience yet, have people on your current staff take the tests to establish a norm, so you can process applicants in a reasonable amount of time. Otherwise, some applicants may spend hours taking tests, while others complain you did not give them the same amount of time.

Be sure everyone is treated exactly the same when you administer tests and give results. Tests should be taken in a quiet place where someone can observe the applicants. Explain the tests and make certain the applicants understand what they are to do. Let them know someone will help them if they have additional questions. We put a porcelain bell on the table where applicants took tests so they could ring for help when they needed it.

It's best if one or two qualified employees are responsible for administering and grading tests. Make sure they are trained and perform those tasks in a consistent manner. Whoever administers the tests must be specific with instructions. This will prevent some applicants from using your inefficiency as an excuse for their poor test results. You want to be fair, but you can't be fair if you don't explain tests properly and in the same way to every applicant.

The applicants' attitude toward the tests reveals something about them. We occasionally had people who tested poorly use the excuse that they didn't really try because they didn't think it was necessary to give the test their full attention or they didn't think the test was that important. From our viewpoint, an applicant who makes such a comment is either using a lame excuse for failing a test or telling us he or she decides what is important. Either way the applicant shows a poor attitude.

Always make test results available for applicants and employees to see. It's best to give applicants the results of their tests during the interview. All tests, applications, and other employee information should be kept in individual files that are available to the employees upon request. They are not to be removed, but they can be reviewed in your presence.

COMPANY HANDBOOKS

Company handbooks can be examined by the applicants while they are waiting to be interviewed. Handbooks include your employees' manual and your company handbook. The employees' manual describes important facts and policies about your company. Since an employees' manual is too detailed for an applicant to read, it is best to show it, then direct the applicant's attention to the company handbook because it briefly reviews key elements of the employees' manual and features material that enhances your company's image. If you don't have either of these handbooks yet, put them together before you start interviewing applicants.

The best way to put together an employees' manual is to obtain one from a company you admire and study it. See how it fits your company's goals: what you believe; what you want to do; your attitude toward vacations, paid holidays, employee benefits, incentives, jury duty, leaves of absence, and other employment issues, including pay incentives and production bonuses. Don't copy. Instead, use the borrowed manual to help formulate your own manual.

When you have put together the material, have it neatly typed, inserted in plastic sheets, and assembled in a three-ring notebook titled "Employees' Manual." The manual should be available for any employee to see. We kept ours in the lunch room along with EEOC, Wage & Hour, and Worker's Compensation Guidelines.

What to Include

Your company handbook should include a brief summary of important policies and any material that features your company in a positive way. Maybe you don't have any accolades you can show or commendation letters from customers or advertising sheets of your product, but you can define your marketing goals and tell something about your company and what you intend to do. Present this information in the same manner as the employees' manual but in a separate three-ring notebook. It should also be available for employees to see. We proudly displayed ours in the lunch room.

Here are some of the things we put in our company handbook: what we are, what we are not, what we do, who we need, our organization policy, our basic rules about smoking, our policy on attendance and attitude, the dress code, a description of warnings and termination procedures, a brief description of work shifts, starting base rates for pay, how pay is calculated, how promotions and bonuses are earned, and information about contests and awards and our benefits, including our pension plan and profit-sharing plan.

We concluded our company handbook with pictures of our product, awards we received from government agencies and industry associations, and commendation letters from vendors and customers.

The major purpose of a company handbook is to make a favorable impression on those who read it. Whether your audience is a customer, a vendor, an investor, or an applicant, you want to make the best impression you can on these people. They are all important to you in one way or another.

If you have a good company handbook for applicants to examine while waiting for their interview, they will have more confidence in your company, and a more positive attitude toward the job, and they will be more eager to work with you.

INTERVIEWS

The *interview* has a major purpose: for you to learn as much about an applicant as possible in as short a time as possible. What goes on during that time determines whether or not you hire that person.

No one is infallible when it comes to evaluating people. That's why most companies use several people to interview candidates. However, in most cases, the interviews are conducted separately. Our company was small. We didn't have the luxury of a personnel department nor the time for applicants to be interviewed separately, so we used the team method.

Team Interviewing

If you are just starting your business and you are hiring your first person, don't interview alone. Invite someone to sit in on the interviews with you, someone you trust who has been successful at hiring good people. If that person does nothing more than witness what transpires during the interview, it's worth it.

It sounds intimidating to have several people question an applicant during an interview. Actually, it's more natural and spontaneous because interview questions are asked in distinct ways by different people. One person interviewing an applicant can sound like a trial attorney interrogating a witness.

Even though the same basic questions are asked in each interview, they can be asked casually by different interviewers who are present. We found it very effective since some people respond better to certain people than to others. The objective is to have a conversational-type interview that is goal directed.

After introductions, use the first part of the interview to show applicants the results of their tests. Make sure they understand what they did correctly and incorrectly. Be specific; don't hedge or you'll give the impression you evaluate people on some nebulous basis and hire people because you "like them."

If they argue with you, remain calm. Do not debate with them or defend your tests. Point out their results again and move on to another subject. You have already learned something about them based on how argumentative they are and under what circumstances they feel you have been unfair. Everything that occurs during an interview reveals something about the people you are evaluating.

The first questions should relate to a person's past employment. Prior to the applicant's entering the room, have everyone look at the application and the tests. We usually began by saying, "Of all the jobs you've had, which one did you like the most?" and then continued with the following:

"What did you especially like about it?"
"Was there anything you didn't particularly like?"
"Which of the jobs did you like the least?"
"What was there about it you didn't like?"
"Was there anything you did like about it?"

Listen to the replies and respond to them. If you ignore them and continue your list of questions you will learn nothing. If any reply suggests a subject needs probing, do so. For example, if applicants say they liked the people, ask in what way and why? If they didn't like the people, ask, "Why is that?" or "How come?" Fit your language style to the applicant's.

Usually, the longer people talk about themselves and the more relaxed they become, the more apt they are to be truthful about problems and relationships with coworkers and employers. Watch their body language. When they answer, do they look at you or look away? Are they tense when you probe certain areas of their work history? Do they exhibit signs of impatience with facial expressions or by shaking their feet or drumming their fingers?

Continue, "If we were to call one of your employers, how do you suppose they would describe you?" Assure them you will not call if they are currently working there. Applicants are usually candid and describe themselves as they think the employer would.

Determining Strengths and Weaknesses

One of the primary goals of the interview is to find out what weaknesses and strengths an applicant has. A number of questions need to be answered. Will this person work well with our people? What kind of attitude does this person have toward the job, toward employers, and toward work in general? Is this person a union organizer who will try to disrupt the labor force?

Before you attempt to uncover weaknesses, discuss a person's strengths. "All of us have strengths and weaknesses in our character. What do you think one of your strong points is?" If they can't think of any, rephrase the question, "Well, what good things do people usually say about you, for example, your parents, a teacher, a friend, or an employer?" That will elicit some response.

You have now laid the groundwork for uncovering the applicant's weaknesses. Say, "You know we mentioned that all of us have strengths and weaknesses and we've talked a little about your strengths. Now we would like to know, what are your weaknesses?" The applicant usually will not be able to think of any, or will hesitate to tell you. Put him or her at ease by describing one of your own. "Well, for example, I know I have a weakness. I tend to talk too much" (or whatever it is). An applicant will usually relax and describe at least one weakness.

If the person still can't think of any, or won't tell you, continue with, "Well, for example, if you were going to a self-improvement course, not a body-building course, but a course to improve your character, what would you elect to improve about yourself or the way you think?" This will almost always elicit an answer.

We had a list of basic questions we asked in every interview. We memorized them and rotated asking them in a conversational manner. Here's another one we always asked: "Of all the things you've done in your life up to this point, what are you the proudest of having achieved? Something you've done personally?" The purpose of that question is to learn what makes them feel proud and good about themselves.

We found we had to add "other than having children," when we interviewed women, because they invariably answered, "having a baby," or "raising my family." Men never said this—with one exception. One young man answered, "Helping my wife deliver our baby with the Lamaze method two hours ago." This was so unusual, I sent it to *Reader's Digest*. It was published in the August 1986 issue under "All In A Day's Work."

Questions You Can and Can't Ask

When we asked applicants about their former bosses, we asked, "Is there anyone you prefer we not call?" They usually said no, leaving us free to call anyone. If you ask for specific people to call or not call, you limit their permission to those people you enumerated. If you ask the question the other way, you are free to call anyone.

You cannot ask applicants if they have a disability, are taking drugs, have been arrested, or have AIDS. You can ask if they have any impairment that would keep them from performing the requirements of the job. If your quality standards are high enough and strictly enforced, workers with poor attitude, attendance, or performance will automatically be terminated for those reasons. You will avoid problems with drugs or other negative issues that worry employers today. We never had a problem, and we never resorted to spot checking or drug testing.

Here are other questions you might adopt. Use them in a conversational manner—*not* as they are listed below.

"If you could do something over again, what would it be?"

"How would your boss describe you as a worker?"

"How would you describe your boss?"

"If you could change anything about your last job, what would it be?"
"Why?"
"Define a 'good job.'"
"How do you react to constructive criticism?"
"How do you react to changing tasks?" "To repetitive tasks?"
"What are your goals for the next five years?"
"How many days did you miss last year at work (school)?"
"What kind of grades did you get in school?"
"Were you ever responsible for the performance of others?"
"Did you ever have to organize or lead others?"
"Do you think you work better alone or with somebody?"
"Is there anything you wish I had asked?"
"Are there any questions you would like to ask me?"

There are reasons for each of these questions. If you present them in a conversational manner and explore each one in depth, you'll learn what you need to know. Always ask open-ended questions that must be answered with more than a "yes" or "no." Otherwise, you'll learn nothing. No matter what questions you ask or how many, always conclude with questions that give applicants the opportunity to tell you more and to question you in return.

Talking about Your Company

When you are finished questioning them, tell them about your company and what you expect of them, referring to the handbook they have just seen. I will describe what we said because I believe it was the basis for our successful management.

One of us in the interview would begin by saying, "We emphasize two things here. One is *good attendance* and the other is *good attitude*. We insist on good attendance because we are a very small company. If you're not here we miss you. We have certain goals and deadlines we have to meet every day in each department. If you're not here we don't meet them, and you don't get a full paycheck.

"To help you have good attendance and a full paycheck, we ask you to make doctor's appointments and social engagements after hours or on Saturdays. If a crisis should arise and you have to miss a day, we ask that you make up the time. Although, let me add, even though you make up the time, it's never the same because we've already missed our goals for that period. It helps, but it isn't as good as being here when we need you the most.

"The other thing we emphasize is a good attitude. The reason we ask you to have a good attitude is that it is more pleasant to work with people who are congenial. If you have a problem at home, we ask you to leave it at home. If you have a problem that is work-related, we ask you to bring it to your supervisor immediately. She can do something about it. Coworkers can't.

"We ask you to try to keep a happy face and a good attitude because if you tell your troubles to the person next to you, it causes more trouble. First of all, they can't help you. Second, you only distract them from their work. Third, they have their own set of problems and don't need yours too. Fourth, when you complain and carry your problems to other people, it affects them negatively and they begin to feel down, too.

"Haven't you ever had the experience of feeling really good when you got up in the morning and then somebody comes up and starts unloading on you and then you feel down? You're kind of depressed and think, 'Golly I felt so good this morning. I wonder what happened?'"

When we say that, everyone agrees, "Yes, I've had that happen to me." Many times, applicants tell about similar experiences they have had. We let them talk about it because it reinforces what we believe—a negative attitude spreads. It also reinforces the policy that when they have work-related problems they are to bring them to their supervisor—not to their coworkers.

Be specific about the policies you feel most strongly about. Make certain they understand those policies and what is cause for probation and termination. (We specified 5% limits for tardiness or absenteeism. We averaged about 1% or 2%.)

Company Policies

Tell them about the other policies. We told them about the dress code, not leaving the premises on the night shift, no personal phone calls, and no smoking policy. We justified the no smoking policy by saying we had to maintain an exceptionally clean environment because of the materials we used in production. We said if they needed to smoke to go outdoors on breaks or during the lunch hour.

We made sure they knew the rule applied to everyone, including visitors.

When we described the dress code, we told them to dress so that none of us would be embarrassed if a visitor took a tour. We had important clients visit occasionally, and we had to maintain an impressive work environment. We also prohibited shoes that were hazardous at work. Our dress code was slightly different for the office. The office employees could not wear jeans or high heels over two inches. Whatever your dress code, be specific, be consistent, be fair, and be sure *you* keep the dress code, too.

We provided an employee telephone so our workers could make calls during breaks. We explained why they couldn't take personal phone calls during working hours except for emergencies. Whatever your policies, describe them and explain why.

The interview is not complete until you have given a description of all the employee benefits, the pay scale, incentives, and other information you emphasized in the company handbook. It's a good way to see whether they read any of it. You can introduce some of the subjects and see how they respond.

Giving a Tour

After the interview, have someone whose opinion you trust give the applicant a tour. This is an opportunity to see the applicant in a situation outside the interview and to assess the person's behavior in relation to other people working for you. We had one of our employees, whom we trained to assess body language, give the tour. She gave the same tour the same way to every applicant. Although it was a quick tour, she pointed out different departments and what they did. She also pointed out safety features such as fire extinguishers and exits, so the applicant would know we provided a safe place to work.

Some applicants behave quite differently when they leave the interview and follow someone they think is unimportant. Some make smart remarks, complain, dawdle, or display aggressive behavior. Others show interest, ask questions, and show enthusiasm. All this is reported by the tour guide to the interview panel, and it contributes to the overall impression of the applicant.

Concluding the Interview

After the applicant returns, conclude the interview by saying, "We have a number of applications on file from people who came in before you. While we try to be as fair as we can and match people's abilities with the right job, we call applicants in chronological order. If the person isn't home or if their line is busy or an answering machine comes on, we go to the next applicant's number. Consequently someone who came in after you might be called before you or you might be called before someone who came in prior to your visit." We found that saying this avoids claims of unfair hiring practices.

CALLING FORMER EMPLOYERS

Calling former employers is an important part of the hiring process. It is difficult to get information from former employers because laws are strict about what former employers can say. Most former employers will give only the dates of employment, salary, and nothing more. (You should do the same if someone calls you about a former employee. Tell the caller to send a written form by mail with the applicant's signature permitting you to give specific information.)

Since you recognize the need to be careful when discussing former employees, you can understand why former employers will be careful when discussing their former employees with you. It is best if you do the calling yourself or have your best manager do it. Whether you or someone else makes the calls, always have a checklist so you don't forget something you want to ask. And always sound as natural and unhurried as you can.

If you have other people make the calls, let them hear you do it several times first; then have them practice with you. Listen to their first few calls. Always follow up with an evaluation review of your calls and their calls so each of you can continue to improve.

Handling the Call

When you call former employers, introduce yourself and explain why you're calling. Ask if they remember the applicant. "I know it's difficult to remember people, but I'd like to ask you a couple of questions. Naturally, I will keep confidential what you say. You see, we like to work with people's strengths and help them with their weaknesses, so it's important for us to know as much about them as we can so we can help them.

"When we interview applicants, we like to know something about them because it makes it easier for us to work with them if we decide to hire them. In our interview we always ask people what their strengths and weaknesses are. Mary said her strength was (whatever it was) and her weakness was (whatever it was)."

If you have expressed yourself in a relaxed manner, the former employer will usually make a remark about the person's strengths and weaknesses. If the person doesn't, add, "Was Mary's description of herself pretty accurate?" At this point the former employer will either agree or disagree. The secret to getting good, honest evaluations from former employers is to get them to relax and to trust you. They must feel what they say will be kept in confidence, so keep a conversational tone and don't hurry them.

Part of learning how to gather information is learning how to listen for cues. For example, if you suggest, "Well, why did a person do such and such?" and former employers answer you immediately, you can be sure it's an honest answer and there is nothing to hide. If they hesitate or can't find the words to express themselves, you may not get an honest answer. Or it may indicate there is more there, and they are fearful of disclosing it. Anything they are fearful or hesitant to disclose implies something negative. If you are uncomfortable about a conversation with someone regarding an applicant's background, don't hire that person.

The last question I always asked former employers was a long one, but I felt it had to be delivered in the right way or I wouldn't get an honest answer. Here's what I said: "You know with all the problems we have with our employees at different times, I have to admit when all is said and done, most of them I would probably hire again. Then there are a few that I say to myself it wasn't worth all the trouble. You know what I mean?" I would give the person time to talk about the statement or to agree in his own words. Then I would continue, "Well, from that standpoint and your work with (use the first name of the applicant) do you think you would hire her again?" Wait for him to say something. You can tell by the way he responds or doesn't respond or how fast he responds what he really feels about that person as an employee.

We seldom bothered to call applicants' personal references because we found it was a waste of time. Applicants generally give references they know will say what they want them to say. Call them only if you are unable to call any former employers.

DECIDING WITH CAUTION

Making the decision to hire the right people is the most difficult part of the process. If you have examined their applications and tests carefully and have conducted a thorough interview, you already have a pretty good idea of whether or not you are going to hire them. Calling former employers either supports the opinion you formed during the interview or it doesn't.

Evaluating the Applicant

The best time to evaluate an applicant is immediately after the interview. Ask the person who gave the tour to join you and get her opinion. Have her describe the applicant's attitude and behavior during the tour. Was there something negative that occurred outside the interview, something no one saw during the interview? Ask if someone in your organization recognized the applicant. Explore anything that might have an effect on your evaluation.

We evaluated applicants on two factors in addition to their ability to perform the basic requirements of the job. You may want to do the same. One factor was the applicant's overall personality and how we thought the person would fit in with us. The other factor was how we thought he or she would be as a worker to manage.

Sometimes you like a person's personality but feel the individual might not fit the kind of job you have available or might not work well with the other employees or might be difficult to manage.

Some people work well with their hands. Other people are good organizers. Still others have all those qualities but are very temperamental. For these reasons, be very careful making a decision to hire someone. You are inviting that person to join your family—your work family.

You can work with temperamental people, but you must have a

job in which they can function without disrupting your work force. We had one employee who was very talented but easily upset. We found that when we put her in inventory control and communicated with her by written memo rather than constant verbal interruptions, she did very well. We told her she was on probation and it had to work. It did.

You must all agree that the applicant has all the qualifications you seek, including a good attitude, before you hire that individual. If any of the interviewers is hesitant or feels uncomfortable about the applicant, you should not hire that person. If you have intuitive bad feelings about a person, let that guide you. Years of experience have taught me to follow my instinct.

Involving Supervisors and Managers

Supervisors and managers were the interviewers in our company. I made certain they knew that the people they hired would be ones they would have to manage or might have to manage. They were far more careful making the decision to hire someone when they knew they might have to manage that person. If any one of the supervisors in the interview felt he or she could not supervise an applicant or would have great difficulty supervising an applicant, we did not hire that applicant at that time.

Sorting it All Out

We never regretted not hiring someone, but we sometimes regretted hiring someone. You can't be too careful, especially today when there are people who would take advantage of you if they could. Your main job during the hiring process is to sort out the bad apples.

Your other job at this stage is to be sure you hire people on the right basis. If you are very specific about your job requirements, very fair in administering all your tests, very clear when you give results, and very assertive in your behavior, people will take you and your company seriously, and you will automatically sift out some bad characters. Even if a couple slip through your hiring process, you will screen them out during the training period—if you do that job properly.

After you have interviewed an applicant, examined his tests and application, and checked his former work history, you are ready to make your decision. If you feel his qualifications best fit the position available, and checking with former employers supports your opinion, hire him.

Never tell the applicant the day you interview him that he is hired. We found that doing so leaves the impression that you are desperate. All the pressure is on you for the applicant to succeed. You want him to want the job badly enough to feel he is lucky to be hired and to feel some pressure himself to succeed. Therefore, always wait at least twenty-four hours before notifying applicants they have been hired.

Call back and say you would like to give the person a try. Tell him what the starting salary will be, what time to come, how he is to dress, and who he is to see upon arrival.

4.

How to Train the Right People

It is important that you believe in new recruits from the start. You must want them as employees; and just as important, they must want you as an employer. If one of these elements is missing at the beginning, the relationship is doomed sooner or later.

Too often, companies spend all their energy and money on the selection process and almost none of it on the training process. You can select potentially ideal employees and then ruin them if you do not give adequate training. On the other hand, you can hire ordinary people and develop them into extraordinary employees if you give the right training.

If you have done everything right so far—recruiting, testing, interviewing, and selecting the right people—they are now hired on the right basis and ready to start their training. Your biggest job is to make certain employees are adequately trained.

Training the new employee is a big responsibility. How well you do it determines her success and yours. You will do it right if you focus on: (1) orientation, (2) initial training, (3) supervisor's role, (4) coworker's role, (5) employee's responsibility, and (6) management's responsibility.

ORIENTATION

Orientation means introduction. It is a reminder that first impressions are the most important. The first day is the most critical day in an employee's life with your company. What you do or don't do, what you say or don't say, how you respond or don't respond, makes a lasting impression and affects the basic attitude of that employee for the duration of employment with your company.

If you leave new employees standing around unattended for any length of time, you and your company give a bad impression. They will think you don't care about them, that you have forgotten them, that you are disorganized or worse, unorganized, or that you don't know what to do with them.

On the other hand, if you have their first day structured so they receive attention, are taught what to do, have things explained and questions answered, and are kept busy, you and your company make a good impression. The trainees will know that you care about them, that you are aware of their needs, that you are well-organized, and that you work at a steady pace.

Their orientation should include another tour of your facility, a review of the rules and regulations, and discussion of the awards the company has received and special benefits they will receive as employees of your company. Tell them about company contests and awards and any other motivational programs your company has. I have described ours in a later chapter. You may want to incorporate some of them in your company's program.

If you have an accountant who handles all employee benefits, make certain the new people see the accountant before the end of the first day so they can fill out the proper government forms. Before you take them to the accountant, review the employee benefits you offer. Make certain they understand. If they have a specific question you can't answer, refer them to your accountant and alert the accountant.

Orientation isn't just meant for new employees. It's for anyone being introduced to a new job. When we trained employees for different positions, we were careful to introduce them to the new job by having them watch others first. It was especially important to do this with new supervisor trainees. (See Figure 3.)

INITIAL TRAINING

Initial training is meant to set the pace. It is very difficult to find and hire good people. Once you have hired them, the most important job you have is to train them right. It is the single most important thing you can do to ensure that you will have good employees and that they will have a good job. Don't waste those precious few days. Make the most of them by doing your best and making sure everyone in your

Figure 3
TRAINING THE NEW SUPERVISOR

As we hire a new person we talk to her on her first day to go over the rules and benefits again in detail and tell her what we will expect from her and what she can expect from us. Since we are training a new supervisor, the plant manager and I decided to have her observe the orientation of a new employee.

Beforehand, we called the supervisor trainee in and told her what we were going to do with the new employee and that we do this with each new person, just as we did when she was new. We let her know she would sit in on orientation sessions when she is training anyone for her department, so we wanted her to know about it now and how we do it.

The plant manager carefully explained all the things that she goes over with new employees and why it's important that these things are pointed out to them their first day. At that point, we called in the new employee and went over everything with her including the typed list the plant manager has that includes important features of the employee manual. I had added bathroom and lunchroom rules to the list.

I think it gave our new supervisor trainee a good feeling to see how we talk to each new employee to make them feel good their first day at work. She also saw how we tell new employees what to do when they have a problem. I felt it was good training for our new supervisor trainee to be in on the orientation of a new employee.

company does his or her best to help get the new employees off to a good start. No effort you make will be as richly rewarded as your training program for new employees.

Have a new employee start at the beginning of the week and the beginning of the shift if you can. When she arrives, have her report to the plant manager or office manager and take her to an office where her supervisor and the manager can review the rules for fulfilling the basic requirements of the job. Make certain she understands you have a probationary period in which she must meet the standard requirements of the job.

Describe Job Requirements

Whatever your requirements are, be specific about them so the trainee knows what is expected of her. Trainees fail most often because of poor training. They don't know what is expected of them. That is because most managers have not given enough thought and planning to setting a standard and expecting others to meet it. After you are certain she understands the basic requirements of the job and her responsibilities during the training period, tell her again about your dress code and other company rules, including those affecting discipline and termination.

When we started our business we said there would be no smoking inside the building. We had no trouble enforcing the rule because we were firm and we were fair. The rule applied to everyone in the plant and the office. Even visitors—from vendors to bankers—could not smoke in the building.

Trainees should know everyone receives the same training for the same type of job. This lets them know that you have no favorites and that rules are equally applied. Emphasize the importance of your policy for good attendance and good attitude and how their response to it can affect their success with your company or with any company they work for later.

Who Will Do the Training?

Let a trainee know she will be trained on the job by a qualified worker. Make sure she knows who her trainer is. That person may be her supervisor, a special trainer, or a coworker from her department or another department.

Tell her that because you are a small company, workers need to know how to do more than one job, so that if business declines and there isn't enough work in the particular department, they can move to another department to avoid being laid off. Explain that the more job skills a worker acquires, the more valuable she becomes and the more money she can make by acquiring additional skills.

Pay and Lay-Offs

At this point do not guarantee there will never be a lay-off. No one can guarantee that, especially a small business. Instead, let her know you care and want to help guard against having to lay anyone off. That's why you want everyone who works for you to be able to perform more than one job. Let new employees know how they benefit from training for different jobs.

During initial training go over the pay scale again. Make certain the trainee understands what her starting pay is, how she may earn more, and what the minimum requirements are for the job she will have. It's a good idea to have her repeat it back to you in her own words. If you let her nod in agreement or mumble yes, you can never be sure she really understood. Later, if she is confused or upset over her pay or the minimum requirements to keep the job, she may think you never told her. If you do these basic things correctly, you can avoid an unemployment claim later. Most unemployment claims are the result of misunderstandings, which are themselves a result of poor communication.

Conclude by letting the trainee know you selected her over other applicants, and you believe she can have a successful career with your company if she tries as hard as the company will. Describe the specific duties and responsibilities of her department. Have the supervisor outline this for her before taking her to her department.

Assessing During the Training Process

During initial training, you should be able to decide whether or not the applicant will succeed in the job for which she was hired. How long you set for your initial training is determined by the

complexity of your jobs. Most of ours required hand-eye coordination. Sometimes the first day or two was enough. However, most
often it took two weeks or longer to be sure. If your jobs require more
technical training or education, it will take even longer.

If your training is set up properly, you can begin to see which
trainees have exceptional skills and which ones need more attention. You can't be with them every minute, but you can let them
know you are available when they have questions or problems.

Our work was so highly skilled that it was often necessary for a
supervisor to demonstrate certain techniques to workers as they
progressed to different levels of expertise. During the training period
it is difficult to know how fast each worker will attain a certain skill
level. If you can develop a method for giving individual attention
and yet not hover over trainees, you will save yourself time and give
them a sense of independence.

We used a bell for each worker in certain jobs that required help
occasionally. Our employees knew if they rang the bell a supervisor
would quickly come to answer a question or give them additional
help. We also had name plates at each worker's station. This helped
everyone get acquainted rapidly and established a friendly atmosphere.

Sometimes, you find trainees have an impairment that keeps
them from fulfilling the requirements of the job, although during the
interview they told you they had none. Give them ample opportunity to correct or improve the impairment. If they cannot, terminate
them. If this happens to you several times, it indicates that you are
not describing the requirements of your jobs accurately enough, and
you need to review your hiring practices. You will have to pay an
unemployment claim for the short time they worked for you because
the mistake was yours for hiring them. Remember, if someone is
terminated for reasons within her control, that is her error. If she is
terminated for reasons not within her control, it is *your* error.

We had this happen to us on several occasions. The women could
not see the fine details of the work they had to do. We gave them
ample opportunity to get new glasses. Sometimes it worked. Sometimes it didn't. If they still could not perform the job, we tried them
on other jobs if we had other jobs available. If not, we terminated
them. We had to change our description of the basic requirements

of the job to include good eyesight so this wouldn't happen again because it was costly and unpleasant for everyone.

When trainees are good and willing workers but unable to do any of the jobs you have available, it hurts to let them go, but it is necessary if you are going to be fair to the other workers. You cannot keep workers who cannot do the job. It is unfair to the other workers, and you set a bad example of not enforcing company standards equally.

We tried working with the handicapped and were unable to utilize any of their skills in our company. All our jobs required quick movement, good hand-eye coordination, or strength and agility. Your company's requirements may be less demanding physically. If you have any work you think the handicapped can perform, it's a good idea to give them a chance by contacting local agencies that work with handicapped persons.

If your jobs require more than average skill, you will find you need to extend the initial training. We felt two weeks was enough. The basic training took about three months. During that period, workers decided whether they *wanted* to do the job, and we decided whether we thought they *could* do it.

If they succeeded during the three-month basic training period, they were eligible for our company benefits and became a permanent part of the company. However, they were still striving to achieve the skills they needed to perform at a level we required. This often took an additional six months for some jobs and an additional nine months for others.

SUPERVISOR'S ROLE

The *supervisor's role* is the most important one. The supervisor's attitude, behavior, and general demeanor set the standard for his or her department and for the company. The department and the people in the department will be no better than the supervisor running it. The major role of a supervisor is maintaining a good relationship with all the workers. That relationship begins with the initial training, when new people are most eager to please and try hardest to emulate those around them.

In a small business, the supervisors are more effective if they are *working* supervisors. They should spend the majority of their time performing the various jobs required of their departments—not isolated in an office. Our supervisors had their own offices, but they were in them only intermittently.

Supervisors work alongside the people they manage. They help train every person in their department. They inspect the work their employees produce, keep the records for their departments, and handle all minor questions and problems that develop in their departments. They are part of a crew that works together to solve problems through good communication.

Training Reports

A part of that communication is *training reports*. These should be kept daily by the supervisor with copies for the senior managers. The reports should be specific, telling what the trainee has learned or is having difficulty learning.

You should have a probationary period for trainees to acquire the basic skills of the job. It should be segmented by time periods. Training reports should be scheduled to reflect those time periods, so the trainees know how they are doing during each segment of their training in the probationary period.

The more specific you are with your requirements, the easier it is to terminate those who don't succeed. They will understand they did not meet your standards. People are not upset when they understand what is happening to them. People only get upset when they feel they have been treated unfairly.

The reports should reflect the trainees' abilities and attitude toward the job. You want to know both their strengths and weaknesses—especially their weaknesses—because you have to work with them and adjust to them.

The most common mistake companies make is ignoring or refusing to report people's weaknesses during training. If you don't report them, you can't take action to help them. Later, if they don't improve, you will have difficulty disciplining them and even more difficulty when you fire them. How can you fire them for not improving when you never told them they needed to improve? They will be confused and angry. Who can blame them?

In our company, we also had trainees write training reports on themselves. The trainer's report was titled, "What I Taught." The trainee's report was titled, "What I Learned." After we initiated this procedure for training reports, we soon discovered what we *thought* we taught was not always what the new person thought he or she learned. If you use this training technique, you may be surprised at the results. It's a good way to check the quality of your training. (See Figure 4.)

Having workers write training reports on themselves prepares them to write time studies on themselves. They establish the habit of writing reports and are better equipped to help with time studies. We never wrote time studies on our workers. We had them do it for themselves. At first they were hesitant and felt they couldn't do it. When we explained they only needed to write down the time as they began a different set of related tasks, they quickly acquired the skills and wrote very good time studies on themselves.

We required time studies on every job every six months. We used time studies to help set the standards for jobs. The studies were especially important when workers changed jobs. Whenever this occurred, we required time studies for the first two to four weeks, depending on the complexity of the job. They used the time study that had been established for the job and entered their own time differences for those same duties. It taught them how to do a time study for particular jobs, and it was a good way for them to check their efficiency. (See Figure 5.)

In addition to writing training reports and time studies, we had our workers keep records of their production, the amount of product they used for each series of tasks, and other information we needed to compile our production schedules and reports. We found with good training and vigilant supervision, they were able to write these reports. It helped us and it helped establish mutual trust.

As trainees are being taught their jobs, they need to be tested. Most often this can be done orally, although written tests are sometimes more effective and give a permanent record for employee files. Even after initial training, new employees should be observed to see how they are utilizing the skills they have acquired.

Figure 4
TRAINING REPORTS

I taught

1. _____
2. _____
3. _____
4. _____
5. _____
6. _____
7. _____

Comments (i.e., problems or questions):

Signature _____ Date _____

I learned _____

1. _____
2. _____
3. _____
4. _____
5. _____
6. _____
7. _____

Questions I have:

Problems I had:

Signature _____ Date _____

Figure 5
TIME STUDY

Name: Rosanne Saad
Date: January 7, 1991

_____	8:30 - 9:30	Boxes
_____	9:30 - 10:20	Clean closets
_____	10:20 - 10:30	Break
_____	10:30 - 11:30	Applications
_____	11:30 - 12:00	P.O.s, mail items
_____	12:00 - 12:30	Lunch
_____	12:30 - 1:00	Supplies, mail items.
_____	1:00 - 2:15	No charges
_____	2:15 - 3:00	Typing, P.O.s
_____	3:00 - 3:20	Proofread typing
_____	3:20 - 3:30	Break
_____	3:30 - 4:10	Send faxes
_____	4:10 - 4:50	Mail items, file
_____	4:50 - 5:00	Clean up

Miscellaneous items done and times for completion:

_____

_____

_____

_____

_____

_____

Correcting Employees During Training

Training reports and tests automatically include things trainees do correctly and things they do incorrectly. How you correct employees during the training period affects the quality of their work. If you correct their mistakes in a positive way as a natural part of a learning process, they will admit mistakes and correct them. The supervisor might say, "We all make mistakes while we're learning something new," or, "I remember making the same mistake when I trained for that job."

If you act upset or angry with them, or treat each mistake as a major crisis, trainees will not admit mistakes and may even try to hide them when they can. It will be much more difficult for you to help them correct mistakes. Our supervisors, managers, and we as owners freely admitted our mistakes, sometimes vociferously, so all the employees would feel comfortable admitting mistakes when they made them. Our company had to maintain a very high quality standard, and we could not do that if people hid their mistakes. We knew people hid mistakes out of fear. So we tried to create an environment of trust.

It does no good to make workers feel they deliberately did something wrong. It is far more constructive to point out the mistake immediately and quietly, help them correct it, then compliment them on something they did correctly or especially well.

That does not mean you can ignore mistakes or treat them as if they don't matter. You need to confront mistakes immediately, as you need to confront any negative element of your business. But that's the point—confront them. Don't ignore them, hoping the mistakes will go away or won't occur again. Instead, correct them immediately, in an optimistic way, and move on to something positive. Make it a habit to criticize in private and praise in public.

Helping New Employees Feel Welcome

An important part of initial training is to provide companionship for new employees, especially during coffee breaks and lunch hour. We had a company policy that provided for supervisors to have lunch and coffee at the same time as their subordinates. During the initial training, the supervisor, her assistant, or a coworker made a point of staying with new workers to make sure they felt welcome.

Conversation in a relaxed atmosphere can be enjoyable. It can be a time for sharing feelings and ideas and for answering questions and uncovering minor misgivings before they become problems. Every employee problem begins as a question, doubt, or reservation.

Often a question arises about a company policy or about a relationship with a coworker. When an employee makes a statement that indicates confusion or concern, supervisors should always probe deeper to get to the bottom of any negative comments. Asking, "What makes you say that?" is a good way to do this. When the worker tells why, the supervisor can give the facts, and this will satisfy the person. If it doesn't, the supervisor needs to tell the worker she will find a way to resolve it and get back to the worker as quickly as possible. Be concerned about any negative feeling—and be helpful. If a person asks a question and you don't know the answer, say, "I don't know, but I'll find out and get back to you as soon as I can."

When you make a promise to workers, keep it. Get back to them soon. If you can't, stop by and let them know you are still trying to find out, so they don't think you have forgotten or that it wasn't important to you. Remember, anything that is important enough for any worker to mention is important enough for you to resolve.

COWORKERS' ROLE

The *coworkers' role* is also an important one, especially during the training period. Supervisors need help training and running their departments. That's when good coworkers can be most effective. There are several compensations for the coworkers. It helps the coworkers practice their job skills; it gives them an opportunity to learn additional skills, including management skills; it provides them with additional income; and it rewards them with recognition.

Recognition

Coworkers should be paid extra and receive recognition for assisting the supervisor and for training new people. We always paid our coworkers extra for these duties, and we recognized them with announcements in our company bulletin and with titles, such as "assistant" and "trainer."

It's a good idea to establish a program that incorporates coworkers as trainers. It's a way for them to begin learning more about their departments and the company. It's also a way to develop future supervisors. Coworkers in our company knew their supervisors wanted them to learn management skills so they could move on to bigger jobs when the time came.

The attitude and attendance of coworkers are quickly imitated by new employees. If coworkers are happy in their work, keep the company rules, communicate well with one another and with their supervisor, and are eager to help others, the new person will perform in the same manner.

Coworkers can also effect positive changes in the company. When we taught our people to do a certain task, we also let them know that if they came up with a better way of doing something, we wanted to know about it. We gave bonuses for new ideas that improved our company. Every week we presented bonuses at a general meeting.

Coworkers were especially helpful in bringing new ideas from their departments. Some workers are too shy to suggest changes to their supervisors, but they will often mention those things to their coworkers. That's when good coworkers can contribute the most— by helping others, while setting a good example for others to do likewise, when they hear of a good idea to improve the company.

If you award bonuses for new ideas, emphasize that you want to make changes—but through the proper channels. For example, if you are training someone to perform a task in a certain way, the person should learn to perform it that way. Let the trainee know that if he or she discovers a better way of doing something, you want to know about it so you can try the new way, under controlled conditions, in order to evaluate it before introducing it to others. Explain that you also need to know about it so you can reward the person with formal recognition and a bonus for improving the company.

The wrong way to do it is to let people make changes on their own without telling anyone. If that occurs, you can never be certain of what is being done or how it is being done. You can never control your quality or production.

EMPLOYEE'S RESPONSIBILITY

Among the *employee's responsibilities* is keeping the company rules. If you incorporate good attendance and good attitude as rules, you need to emphasize keeping these as the basic responsibilities. Employees also have a responsibility to maintain, to the best of their ability, the standards set by the company. This includes the production standard and the quality standard.

Another responsibility of employees is to support the company goals. Our company had several goals: innovating new techniques and designs; producing an expensive product; maintaining a very high quality standard; and giving prompt service. Our daily goals supported these major ones. Be sure all your employees know what your company's goals are and that they must support them.

The other major responsibility of employees is to share knowledge. If they know you have no secrets, that your policy is one of learning by sharing, they will be more willing to communicate with you. Let employees know they will learn more by teaching others. When they share any bit of knowledge, they are teaching others.

We grow and arrive at generalizations and theories about business when we accumulate knowledge based on experience. Employees should be made aware of their contribution. Their knowledge and experience form the basis of your business.

MANAGEMENT'S RESPONSIBILITY

Management's responsibilities are several. One includes providing the best training with the staff that is available. You have the responsibility of telling new employees what is expected of them and what they can expect from your company. Some trainees are rapid learners; others take longer to acquire the same skills. It's important to let the new worker know you have a production rate and pay scale based on experience with other people who have mastered the same job. You know how long it should take for someone to learn a certain task.

What if you don't know? Admit you don't know, but you do know what it takes for similar jobs, and you are willing to work with the trainee to discover how long the training period should be for a new job, and to adjust the pay scale accordingly. Always be honest with your people and let them know you are trying to do the right thing. This will build mutual trust.

Checking Progress

Tell the trainee how long the probationary period is for learning the job, what the minimum requirements are, and how she can meet them. Keep accurate records of performance and report progress frequently. It's a good idea to have a production board that is visible, so the trainee can chart her own progress. It's also a good motivator when someone is interested in comparing her progress with someone else's.

The trainee should be striving to achieve and to feel good about herself. If she can check her progress against some norm, it will make her feel good to know she can improve each day through her own efforts.

It is management's responsibility to let new workers know how they are doing. They need to know at what level of performance they should be working, for any given period, so they can keep track of their own progress and understand why they are, or are not, getting pay raises. They need to know they control their own pay raises, because pay raises are given objectively—not subjectively. If trainees don't succeed at particular jobs, they need to know what their options are. Can they try another job? Or was that the only one available?

The biggest mistake managers make during training is neglecting to inform workers of their progress. New workers want to do the right thing, but they don't always know what it is. If you don't tell them when they make a mistake, you reinforce the mistake because they don't know they made it and will continue to make it. Any mistake a trained worker repeatedly makes is management's fault. That's why training reports are important.

Good Communication

Establish an atmosphere that invites questions, so you can satisfy employees' qualms or misgivings when they have them. If you make them feel it's OK to ask questions, from the beginning, and foster that feeling for the duration of their employment with you, they will be less likely to cause you trouble. The basic cause of misunderstandings is poor communication.

Workers should feel free to communicate with any supervisor, especially their own, or with other managers. If you establish a friendly, open relationship with everyone, workers will know they can come to you for help and advice. Point out that discussing a problem with someone who can solve it, such as a supervisor or manager, is problem solving. Discussing it with someone who can't solve it, such as a coworker, is counter-productive.

Train new employees to go to the source—supervisors or managers—for information. Otherwise, they will get secondhand information, which is always distorted in some way. You can use the whispering game as an example. Someone starts a message at one end of the room, and it's whispered from one person to the next until it arrives at the original source, completely different.

It is management's responsibility to instill a sense of belonging and enthusiasm in new employees, so they will want to do their jobs well and have a career with the company. They should feel they are joining a happy, well-adjusted group and have a chance to become a valuable part of that network.

Offering Opportunities for Advancement

Another obligation of management is to make certain trainees know about opportunities for advancement. During their training, introduce new workers to employees who have been promoted from entry-level jobs to other positions. Point out supervisors and other managers who have worked at similar jobs when they started.

If you develop your own managers, which is the best way to get good managers, be sure new employees know this. They will be more likely to view your company as a permanent place to work because they will know there are many opportunities for them to grow without changing companies.

Trainees should know the tests they took before they were interviewed were examples of the many tests they may be taking while they work for you. When you have openings for different jobs that require more ability and a broader background, invite everyone to test for those jobs. Have a series of tests to indicate what a person is capable of doing in relation to the jobs you have available. It's always best to develop your own tests pertaining to specific jobs, rather than relying on tests devised by someone who has never worked at those jobs or who doesn't understand your business.

Avoid a multi-level, hierarchical image. Instead, let everyone know you all work together for the same thing—to get a good product (or service) out the door on time at a fair price. If your company includes an office with salaried workers and a production facility with hourly workers, be especially careful to treat everyone equally.

In our company we let workers know they didn't have to remain on a particular job. If they really felt it was going to be a hardship for them because of family responsibilities or they didn't enjoy a particular job, we gave them opportunities to change jobs when different jobs became available.

For example, over the years we hired several young women who were trained as secretaries, but they soon preferred working in our decorating studio on production jobs. Several of these employees' parents wanted their daughters to work as secretaries because of the status they thought it implied. That was why they sent them to secretarial schools. The employees knew that in our company the status of hourly studio production workers was the same as salaried office workers. So they chose the jobs they really enjoyed doing, rather than remain on jobs their parents preferred for them.

Training Back-Ups

Another responsibility of management in a small business is to train back-ups for every job, so that when people move there is less disruption. Our company made sure all employees knew how to perform more than one job. We encouraged them to learn several jobs. We took this a step further by encouraging supervisors to train assistants who could serve as back-ups and eventually take the supervisors' jobs when they moved up.

Nothing is permanent, and if you work with a labor force that is young and in a transitional period of their lives, you need to prepare for change constantly. Managers need to look ahead and train back-ups for every job. If you are a small company, this is the best and safest way to ensure that your business runs smoothly. (See Figure 6.)

Figure 6
UPDATE ON TRAINING IN
THE ACCOUNTING DEPARTMENT

Just to let you know, September is the month that the computer operator is doing some of the bookkeeper's job while the bookkeeper trains the accountant on all the Cado functions. Once successfully completed at the end of the month, we will be able to give the girls the raises that we talked to them about for doing this.

At the beginning of October, I talked to the girls about the accountant learning the computer operator's job, which would be the last thing she would have to learn up there, while the computer operator learns the Cado. This would let the computer operator advance in her knowledge of the accounting department and also enable us to give her a pay raise at that time once she has successfully completed her training.

After that, I think the computer operator should go on the learn more of the bookkeeper's job. That would be in November. So they are set to do these things and at the end of the month we will see how well things run in order to be able to give them their pay raises.

It may appear that our small company was playing musical chairs with jobs. But the results we had from cross-training people in jobs were remarkable. Employees took more interest and felt more secure because they had a variety of things they could do. And they could fill in when needed.

We had a number of young women who held key positions in our company and left for short periods to have babies. In almost every case, they resumed working after two months. There was little disruption in their departments because they had trained back-ups to take their places while they were gone.

Planning for Slack Periods

Managers also have to plan for slack periods by compiling a list of low priority jobs to do during those periods. In our company, we knew our special kiln-firing racks had to be hand-scrubbed sometime during the year. Light fixtures, shelves, and other plant furniture had to be thoroughly cleaned by hand. We had a janitorial service for daily chores, but we preferred to do these special chores ourselves.

We saved those low priority jobs to do during our twice-a-year vacation shutdown. Workers who had not qualified for the week's paid vacation did those chores. Supervisors rotated their vacation schedules to make sure someone was there to supervise the people. It provided a way for the new workers to earn money and a way for us to get the low priority jobs done.

Ongoing Training

Another responsibility of management is to realize that training employees is a permanent part of your business. Whether you are training recruits for a new job or staff members for a change in position, you need to give the same attention to detail. If you establish a structured training program, remaining flexible for changes that occur, you will avoid many problems such as poor attendance, poor attitude, poor workmanship, and poor production, that plague so many businesses.

Operations Manual

A final responsibility of management is to provide a company operations manual. If you haven't started one yet, do it now. Describe every job, what duties each includes, responsibilities, procedures, techniques, training time, production minimum, pay scale and rate, and anything else that pertains to the job.

The best way to know what you must put in the operations manual is to imagine someone coming to learn about your business with no one there to teach them. If you approach it like that, you will probably include the salient features of every job. It is very time consuming to create such a manual, but it is possible if you share the work with every person.

Have everyone write a short description of what he or she does, how it is done, and any other details they can give. Go over the description with them, and observe for yourself what they do to make sure they haven't left out something important. Writing a description of what you do is something like proofreading your own work. It's easy to forget something.

When you have all the information from workers and supervisors, you can go over the material and compile it in the order in which your product or service is produced or conducted. Include diagrams or photographs or both if it makes the book easier to read and understand.

You will need to update the manual continually. It is a never-ending chore but one you must do if you are going to function at a high quality level. You will reap some benefits from it in addition to being better organized. You will have material that supports your statements about job requirements if you are ever checked by a government agency. The manual can be used if you ever need to prove that a terminated worker was not meeting the basic requirements of a particular job.

You may want to develop separate manuals for each machine you have. We had separate machine manuals that included the one supplied by the machine manufacturer and our own revised version. We put additional copies of all our information about each machine in the operations manual. Your machine manuals should provide a complete guide to the operation, scheduling, and maintenance of the machine. You should include your daily, weekly, monthly, or quarterly checklists. We even had one for our copy machine. (See Figure 7.)

Give instructions that include explanations of why procedures are done a certain way. The more detailed you can be about how and why things are done, the easier it is for others to use the same techniques when they write new training procedures. Your job is to set a good example for others to follow.

An operations manual documents what you do, provides an excellent training tool, and acts as a safety check when you or anyone else question any of your methods of operation. It lets others see you are well organized, and it is one more tool that helps provide a predictable environment. It makes good sense to do it.

During the training period you have the opportunity and the obligation to establish mutual trust by setting a good example.

Figure 7
DAILY CHECKLIST FOR COPY MACHINE

At the close of each day:

1. Turn off the copy machine.

2. Total the number of copies made for the day and record the total in the book behind the copy machine. Items that are starred are copies made in blue.

3. Take count off the machine:

    a. Push color key button and number button at same time.

    b. Keep finger on color code key.

    c. Read number of copies made.

    d. Write this number in folder. If different than the number of copies listed, route memo to everyone who uses the machine indicating the number of copies we were off for the day. Put V.P. at top of memo.

4. Check paper in machine and fill if needed.

5. Check toner and fill if needed.

6. Clean glass with glass cleaner and wipe off machine.

7. Prepare next day's information sheet with date, department, items copied, number, and initials.

5.

How to Motivate the Right People

People are motivated for a number of reasons. Enthusiasm is a necessary ingredient, but what motivates some people doesn't always motivate others. However, there are some things you can do to create an atmosphere that motivates your people. Money isn't always the motivating factor. Motivators can include a number of things you do to satisfy employees' basic needs: to feel valued, to feel secure, to feel they can achieve something on their own. If you help satisfy those needs, you will motivate them.

Motivating employees for your small business can be fun and rewarding for all of you. Every day you will see opportunities to motivate others if you are creative. Here are some ideas to consider to help you motivate your employees: (1) be flexible, (2) provide TLC, (3) give awards and bonuses, (4) have contests, (5) review and evaluate, and (6) offer freelance work to employees.

BE FLEXIBLE
Be flexible if you want to motivate people. Your policies stipulate certain working hours for certain shifts and certain wages for certain positions. You need to be fair and consistent when enforcing those policies in order to provide the predictable environment your people require to perform well.

Can you ever make exceptions and let workers schedule their own hours? My experience with our small company suggests you can, in some cases, if you use common sense and evaluate the situation carefully. If you show you are flexible, it will motivate your employees. Here is an example of how we did it in our company.

When our night supervisor was unable to continue working

because of her son's problem in school, we explored the problem with her, found what hours she needed to be with him, and made arrangements for her to arrive at a different time. We kept her pay the same because we knew her worth was in the job she was doing, not necessarily in the number of hours she was working.

I knew several important things about her: she was a dedicated worker, she needed the job, and she was serious about a career with us. I also knew that, like most mothers who work, she felt a deep obligation to her family. Clearly, we had a problem. I never viewed it as *her* problem, I viewed it as *our* problem—the company's, the plant manager's, the supervisors', and mine.

Therefore, I included them in the decision-making process. I knew they would gain first-hand experience solving problems like hers; they would see those problems as our problems; they would know if they had similar problems they could expect the same consideration; and finally, their involvement would give them a sense of *esprit d'corps* and build company loyalty.

Rather than lose our night supervisor as an employee on the evening shift, where she was badly needed, we jointly decided to make an exception and let her schedule her own hours. After some careful planning, here's what we did. First, we asked her how early she could come to work. Next, we asked what arrangements she would make to manage her department until she arrived. Here's what she did: she selected someone who was eager to assume more responsibility and made a checklist for that assistant. She also talked with her evening shift employees and enlisted their help. They were eager to show how they could help by becoming more self-reliant.

We then asked her how long she thought it might take her to work out her family problems. She was honest and said she didn't know, but that she would try to work them out as soon as she could, since she was keenly aware of the faith we placed in her to make such an exception.

Everyone recognized how important it was for her to spend those particular hours with her family. We also recognized how important it was not to lose her as a supervisor on the evening shift. We all agreed that the major priority was for her to continue working in her present position. But what about the pay?

I asked the supervisors if they felt they were being paid mainly because of the number of hours they put into the job or because of their expertise and the responsibilities. They all agreed that they were being paid for their expertise and the responsibilities they had and not necessarily for the number of hours they worked. They saw their main value to the company as "getting the job done no matter what hours were involved."

We mutually agreed that during the time she was resolving her family problems, it would be to everyone's benefit to continue paying her for the job she was doing, despite the different hours.

I did one final thing. I talked with our two company accountants—also career women with homes to manage—to enlist their cooperation. I felt it was important to share this information with them so they would understand, since they were involved with her time cards and paychecks. I explained what we wanted to do and why. They agreed with our decision and trusted our judgment.

From the company's standpoint, the supervisor's value far exceeded the difference in her work schedule. With this solution, she continued to gain more experience as a supervisor. She organized her department so that one of her assistants could take over until she got to work. Her plan provided an opportunity for the workers on the night shift to grow in their jobs and also provided an opportunity for her assistant to develop management skills. The manager and supervisors learned how to deal with problems that face companies and their top managers.

A year later, after the supervisor's son had made his adjustment at school, she asked to return to her full schedule. She appreciated the support we had given her when she needed it. She especially appreciated the effort the company had made on her behalf and worked even harder. Everyone was more motivated because they knew we cared enough to be flexible.

The other exception the company made concerning flexible work hours was for a packer. She, too, had worked for the company a long time (five years) and was an outstanding producer. She had a good attitude, and when her first baby was born returned to work after six weeks.

After her second baby was born, she couldn't return to work because her husband's work shift caused baby-sitting problems. Our company valued her ability with numbers and we decided that while she couldn't work flexible hours as a packer, she was a perfect candidate to work in the decal department taking inventory. It really didn't matter *when* the items were counted, as long as they were counted correctly.

I asked her, "How many hours can you work each day?" and "What hours can you work?" She said she could work eight hours a day but the hours would vary depending on her husband's schedule. Some days she could work from five in the morning to twelve-thirty. Other days she could work from five at night to one in the morning.

I discussed it with the plant manager and supervisors. We all agreed the employee could work the hours she needed and could keep her own time cards. As before, I also discussed our decision with the two accountants and received their support. She did such a good job that she was put in charge of the decal department.

After she was able to return to work on a regular shift, she was promoted to supervisor of the warehouse. The loyalty she felt for the company was reflected in her eagerness to do her best. We reaped an additional benefit. We learned we could communicate by memo with the decal department inventory control clerk. We were then able to put a talented but overly sensitive worker in that job, where she wouldn't have constant verbal interruptions and could perform well.

Both employees appreciated the exceptions we made for their flexible work hours, but we made the exceptions because they were exceptional people. You can make exceptions too, if you are careful. First, make certain that the situation warrants a change. Be sure to include your managers when deciding what to do. After you make your decision, inform those people who need to know and be honest when you discuss it. If you take these precautions you have another way to motivate your people—by being flexible.

PROVIDE TLC

Provide tender loving care for your employees, and they will be motivated to do their best. Good people appreciate what you do for them. What may seem unimportant to you may be very important to someone else. For example, employees who come from families that work at salaried jobs are comfortable working on a salary basis.

Workers who come from families that work at hourly jobs are more comfortable with hourly pay. Try to provide the method of payment with which your employees will feel most comfortable.

Our company was located in a heavily industrialized, union-oriented community. We knew most of our workers came from union families, even the supervisors and top managers I developed. Knowing this, we paid them hourly wages even after they were promoted to supervisor. We knew they were more comfortable with that method of payment.

When I developed senior managers, we put them on salaries but we were careful to show them how they were being compensated and how we were following wage and hour guidelines. We let managers know we would return them to an hourly rate if they preferred it.

Anytime we changed employees' pay from salary to hourly or hourly to salary, we let them know we would return to the other method if they were more comfortable with it. If people know you are willing to accommodate them, they are more willing to try new things because they trust you.

When you pay hourly wages, you make the employees feel more secure, and it gives you another way to show them you aren't taking advantage of them. For example, knowing our supervisors came from union families that mistrust management, I wanted to be more than fair when they stayed even five minutes to discuss a management problem with me. No one can manage and walk out the door every day on time. So here's what we did.

If I asked employees or supervisors to stay for a few minutes after work to discuss something I insisted they be paid overtime. If they stayed five minutes I made sure they were given credit for fifteen minutes. When I had a meeting after work with eight employees that took five minutes, before leaving the meeting I asked our accountant to be sure everyone got paid for fifteen minutes overtime. Everyone knew they had only been there five minutes. I said, "I know we only ran five minutes overtime, but I would feel better if you were paid for fifteen minutes overtime. Then I'm sure we're covered." Be scrupulously fair and honest with your employees regarding their pay. That's TLC—a good motivator.

Keeping Pay Equitable

If you move a worker from one job to another, make sure he receives the same pay or has an increase in pay. While someone is trying a new job make sure his pay doesn't decrease. If he asks to be moved to another department or another job, make sure he knows he has the responsibility to work at the rate that job requires, but while he is learning let him keep his current base rate.

If you are consistently using the training reports and the time studies each time people change jobs, they will know how they are doing and what their responsibilities are to maintain or increase their pay. Your main objective is to make sure they know *they* control their pay—not you.

When you introduce new machines or a new procedure that might increase production, use some tender loving care. Make sure workers are satisfied that their pay won't suffer or that they won't be hurt in other ways, such as losing their jobs. For example, in our company when I mentioned that a machine would quadruple production and a new pay chart would have to be used to adjust for the increase, one employee asked, "Will we be just doing the hard things then by hand?" I answered, "Yes, why do you ask?" Several workers said, "Well, we use the easy stuff to increase our production so that we get more pay that way." "Now we won't have the easy stuff to do for easy money." "We'll only be doing the hard stuff."

Immediately I replied, "I'm glad you brought that up. I want our accounting department to look up the production for the past few months and identify how much of your pay was due to the easy stuff. We'll show you. And we'll make sure that whatever percentage it represents and whatever the dollar amount it represents will be maintained on your paycheck. That way you will be protected by our adding that much to your production pay.

"In other words, you will be assured of making at least as much as you made before, but the work will be easier on the machine. You'll probably make more because you'll do the easy stuff faster and have more time to spend on the hard stuff that pays more. We'll increase the rate for that portion, too, because the machine will make us more profitable, and we can afford to pay you more for the hard stuff."

I went a step further with TLC. I added, "I want to make sure all of you are comfortable with this. So let's get together again when the new machine is in production and jointly we'll set up what you think is fair." Everyone left the meeting satisfied—not fearful. They were looking forward to the new machine and their new pay increases.

Notice that when I talked with them I did not use fancy words. When you have meetings with your employees don't talk over their heads. On the other hand, don't talk down to them. They are more likely to feel comfortable with you and communicate with you if you adjust your language style to fit theirs. Here is another example.

Solving Problems

When we had a serious quality problem with a very expensive line of hand-painted porcelain gift items, I discussed it with the supervisors. We called a meeting with the employees who were involved and showed them the production figures, including the high losses (98%) and the cost. We planned what we were going to say ahead of time because we knew the meeting was important. We used an analogy they could relate to.

"If any of you went to the grocery store and bought steak at $4.00 a pound from your butcher and got it home only to discover that he had given you $1.98 hamburger, what would you do?" They all said, "I would take it back immediately and demand my money back," "I would not do business with him again," "I would show him what he had done and tell him he didn't give me my money's worth."

We explained when we paid them top dollar for top quality and they gave us poor quality, we weren't getting our money's worth. They were doing the same thing as the butcher. Immediately, they understood the point. Then we asked them what they thought we should do. We told them we knew they were good people, and they were not deliberately cheating us. There was no question of demoting them or firing them. The question was really, "How do we get a better quality product through your efforts?"

They jointly arrived at solutions that worked. They suggested a penalty, which we called a production adjustment ratio, that was harsher than I would have devised for them. But it worked.

Each piece they decorated that was not useable and had to be discarded was subtracted from their total production count. The value of the piece determined how much was deducted. Some very expensive pieces were given a 5-to-1 ratio. But the employees helped set the ratio. We did not arbitrarily set it. The idea worked and became a company policy for the high quality, expensive items we produced. The workers shared in the problem and in the decision-making process that brought about the solution. Their intimate involvement motivated them to do better.

Managers who are reluctant to share problems with workers are afraid their suggestions may not be good ones. I have found *workers' suggestions are often the best*. They are intimately involved with the problems and usually know things you don't know, which might contribute to the solution.

An example of what can happen when you *don't* include workers in problem-solving sessions occurred in the huge factory I studied years ago. For several weeks, they had been losing whole cartloads of mustard lids in the forming department and couldn't figure out why.

One day when I was in the drug store visiting with a worker from that department, I asked how things were going at work. He told me a careless worker was hitting the cart containing mustard lids each night and breaking them. I asked him to tell management about it. He said he had been trying for two weeks, but no one would listen to him. Every time he approached some supervisor or manager he was told, "Not now, I'm going to a management meeting." The worker told me, "You know what? I think them [sic] guys have too many management meetings." I knew their problem wasn't management meetings. Their problem was ignoring their workers.

Ask for Suggestions

Don't be afraid to ask workers for suggestions. If you have ideas you want to suggest, you can interject them within *their* ideas by saying, "How do you think this might work?" Then give the suggestion. You want them to be a part of the decision-making process because they will have a vested interest in making it work. Taking the time to include employees in problem-solving sessions, and explaining problems in ways employees can relate to, are other examples of TLC and good motivators.

Rewards

TLC can take the form of monetary bonuses. Sometimes what is important isn't the amount of money you give, it's the thought behind it. We made it a practice to give money and a birthday card to employees and to give valentine cards and candy, Easter eggs, a small Christmas gift, money for a turkey at Thanksgiving, and donuts when we knew we were working overtime or the weather was especially dreary. Sometimes we had no excuse. We just felt like supplying donuts as a surprise. When you do thoughtful things for others at work that's TLC and a good motivator. Sometimes our workers would bring homemade goodies to share with everyone. We never asked them to, nor did we expect it. But they were motivated to reciprocate each time we did something for them.

Sending employees to industry seminars or management meetings is another good way to motivate them. Anytime you invest additional dollars in them you build trust. They know you care about them and believe in their abilities. There is no better motivator than your belief in them.

When you send employees to seminars, tell them what is expected of them when they return. We sent employees to seminars that pertained to their jobs. We paid all their expenses and their wages for a regular work day when they attended. They appreciated it because they knew it was expensive. They also knew they had a responsibility to share what they learned with us. They wrote reports and presented what they had learned at the next meeting so we could all benefit from it. They looked forward to those special days. It gave them an opportunity to show all of us what they had learned. It also motivated others to emulate them.

You may want company picnics, dinners, or parties. They can be good motivators. We had a company picnic each summer and a company party at Christmas. We had three supervisor dinner meetings each year and a luncheon for senior members (anyone who had worked for us two years or more). We also recognized the senior members with a wristwatch with our company logo. Those with ten years' service received initialed gold pen and pencil sets.

We bought fund-raising tickets from local organizations for ball games, circuses, and dances and gave the tickets to employees. The supervisors made sure the tickets were given fairly and rotated among the employees who would use them for themselves and their families.

We bought season tickets to the symphony and invited employees to use them. The tickets were not given as a reward or bonus but as an added gesture to let them know we were thinking of them. We told them we bought the tickets to support the symphony but wanted them to enjoy the tickets. Every month two to four employees attended performances. Most of them had never attended a symphony. Some of them didn't want to go a second time. Others did. They all appreciated our gesture, and a few asked to use the tickets whenever we had them.

Taking an interest in your employees' hobbies can motivate them too. When I discovered one of our secretaries sang in a church choir and dreamed of singing with an opera, I made arrangements for her to audition for the symphony chorus. She was accepted and sang with the symphony chorus that year. Everyone at our company was proud of her achievement and shared in her success.

When our symphony had a formal ball, we bought tickets and invited six of our key people and their spouses to join us. They all appreciated the gesture, and it became a yearly event. These evenings were a way to celebrate working with congenial people, not a reward for doing something special at work. Yet looking forward to the annual ball motivated those employees to do a better job.

You may not want to do what we did, but you can do other things that show your employees you appreciate them. If you think of them as individuals and take an interest in them and what they like, you will think of thoughtful things you can do for them.

At the time we sold our business, we were exploring the possibility of having a day care center for working mothers. Most of our employees had relatives or close friends who were eager to earn money baby-sitting. If your labor force does not have that advantage, you might explore the possibility of providing a day care center for working mothers.

One of the first things I noticed about small industries in the Orient was the number of small companies that had in-house day care centers for the preschool children of employees.

The children were cared for by an employee designated for that job. They were well behaved and secure knowing their mothers were nearby. I was impressed with what I saw, and we vowed to do this someday if baby-sitting became a problem for our employees. You might want to explore it as another way to give some TLC to your work force. It would be a great motivator because it would show your workers you are a caring company.

GIVE AWARDS AND BONUSES

Awards and bonuses can be effective motivators if you present them in the right way. Always make presentations in a general meeting on a Monday—never on Friday. You want the recipients to feel proud all week from what has taken place. It will help to motivate them and everyone in their department.

When you give awards or bonuses, make certain everyone knows what the criteria are. Ask your employees to help you set the goals for awards and bonuses. Our supervisors selected the employee of the month by suggesting a person in the weekly meeting and telling why they felt that person should have the award. The criteria were good attendance, good attitude, and outstanding performance or steady, reliable performance.

We also had a supervisor of the period award in which we recognized the special work or achievement of a supervisor during a six-month period. The plant manager, vice president, president, and myself jointly selected the supervisor based on growth in the job during that period.

If you award bonuses, make certain individual effort is rewarded even if it is a departmental project or a company project. People are more motivated when they know they will be rewarded individually for what they do. They will cooperate and work collectively, but they need recognition for individual effort. They don't necessarily have to compete with each other; they do best when they compete with their own record. They feel proud of what they have achieved and of their improvement.

If you must have them compete with each other, give an award for total production and an award for most improvement. We always did. That way the newest trainee has a chance to win. To be motivated, employees must feel they have an equal chance to win and a chance to feel good about themselves.

If you give awards and bonuses, take pictures and hang them in the lunch room. If you have a company newsletter, put pictures in it. I suggest you have a newsletter in which you announce promotions, awards, bonuses, and anything of interest to the employees.

The supervisors rotated as reporters for our paper, and the secretaries typed it. We made sure they were paid for the time they spent on the company paper.

Our company gave several awards: bonuses for suggestions that improved our company or for reporting mistakes that might hurt our quality or production; an employee of the month award; and a supervisor of the period award. The last two awards consisted of a porcelain plate richly decorated, using a gold border and gold lettering with the employee's name, the date, and the award title.

The plates hung on the wall for the month for the employee of the month award and for six months for the supervisor of the period award. Then the recipients took them home to keep as a permanent record of their personal achievements at work. You may have better ideas. If you can make one of your awards a company product, it will help build company pride and loyalty.

Bonuses are a good way to motivate workers, especially when you need extra effort for a project. If you award bonuses, make sure you plan ahead for the cost, how it will affect your business to justify the bonuses, and how and when you will award them. You need to plan ahead before you make an announcement. Set the parameters, make certain everyone knows and understands, and then make your announcement. Some bonuses can be a permanent part of pay; other bonuses can be given periodically when you need extra effort. Be consistent and be fair. Don't award bonuses across the board.

We never gave bonuses or pay raises as a yearly incentive without a reason. We felt cost-of-living increases were destructive because employees come to expect them even when your business is losing money. We always found reasons to award yearly pay increases and bonuses. We tried to base them on individual performance.

It is more time consuming and takes some planning to award increases based on individual effort, but it pays dividends in employee attitude and motivation. Instead of getting yearly increases because they are at work, they know they get increases because of what they do as individuals when they are at work.

We gave bonuses on production, and we made certain that every award, including our yearly perfect attendance award, was accompanied by a bonus. If you give bonuses on group production, make certain workers are also rewarded for their individual effort.

HAVE CONTESTS

Contests can motivate workers if they compete against themselves and not necessarily against each other. Since our management policy emphasized the individual, we thought it was most important to have contests that rewarded employees for their individual effort.

We took their base rate for production or for the duties they performed, and we used that as we set the criteria for the contest. We asked them to help us set the parameters for themselves and for the contest. We also asked them to tell us what kind of award they thought would be appropriate. The contests are more fun and motivate everyone more if each person shares in the decision-making process.

Your goal should always be to motivate people to be the best they can be for themselves. You want them to improve their performance, not compared with what others do but with what *they* can do. You need to have a standard based on what you know others can do. But beyond that, your contests should be opportunities for self-improvement, not competitions with winners and losers. If you compete with yourself, you are always a winner if you are honestly trying. And that's what you want—to motivate people to try.

You need to give prizes when you have contests. I suggest you give your product if you can. It will save you money and make your people proud to own something they have made. We used our product more often than we did money. We paid bonuses during contests because bonuses were always awarded for production, but for special contests we used our product.

All contests don't have to center on production to motivate employees. The object is to have fun and build enthusiasm among yourselves. We lived in an area that celebrated Halloween, and we had a relatively young labor force. Those who were older were highly creative and enjoyed making costumes for Halloween. We knew they had parties outside work, so we invited them to take pictures of their costumes at their parties and bring them to work.

We had a contest in which we tried to guess who the characters in Halloween costumes were. We had several winners who guessed correctly. We had another contest to vote on the best costume and the scariest costume. We had two winners in that contest. We awarded our product and candy and made announcements with pictures in the company newsletter.

If you have women working for you who are having babies during their tenure with you, have contests to guess the birth date and sex of the new babies. We put a porcelain bank and a sheet for writing our guesses in the lunch room. We signed our names behind our guesses and put a quarter in the bank. After the babies were born, the winners shared the money.

If you have programs like that, be sure you don't coerce anyone to enter the contest. Let them know they are welcome. Our employees or supervisors initiated those kinds of contests, and we joined in the fun.

REVIEW AND EVALUATE

Review and evaluate the performance of your employees at least once a year. They need to know how they are doing on their goals. If you remember, during the interview we asked our applicants, "Where do you see yourself in five years?" We wanted to know if they had goals, what they were, and how we could help them reach those goals.

Setting Goals

When your employees join your company, it's a good idea to find out as much as you can about their goals. The job you provide should contribute to their personal goals in some way. They also need goals at work—goals they set themselves. You need to have them put their goals in writing. It helps them clarify goals and becomes a road map for them. Each year they can pull out their notes to see how far they have traveled on their road to success.

Each year we notified employees one week in advance of a personal meeting to discuss their goals. We wanted to know how they thought they were doing and what they wanted to accomplish in the future. This gave them time to think about it and review what they had said they wanted to accomplish when they joined the company. Employees made notes about what they thought they had accomplished in the context of what they had planned. Their notes also included what they wanted for the future. We had the same kind of review and evaluation for supervisors and managers. We did theirs every six months.

In addition to these annual and semi-annual reviews and evaluations, you may want to have more frequent sessions. One manager I developed had informal review sessions each month. Her sessions with employees consisted of a friendly chat with each one when she gave them their checks.

The employees were paid every two weeks, so every other pay period she would invite each employee to her office where they would pick up their checks and chat with her. It took her all day and evening to dispense the paychecks for our small labor force. While you may not agree with her management style, it worked for her. I did not do it when I worked in her capacity, but she wanted to do it because she felt it was the best way for her to keep close to her people.

You may decide to have a standard yearly evaluation. You can buy stock evaluation sheets. We looked at several but were more comfortable creating our own with our employees. If you use standard evaluation sheets, augment them with questions of your own that pertain to your company and its goals. Leave room for employees to set some goals of their own.

When people evaluated their own performance and set goals, I found they were honest and tended to be more critical of their achievements than I would have been. Here's an example of what we said at one of these meetings. "Well, how do you think you did these past months? Do you remember what it was you wanted to achieve?" They always brought their past goals with them and knew how they had done. After discussing in detail what they felt they had accomplished, we asked, "Well, what would you like to accomplish in the next few months? Where would you like to be?"

We did not limit our conversation to their work. If they wanted to talk about personal goals and how to reach them, we listened and tried to help. We found the review and evaluation process was productive and helped employees focus on immediate goals that supported larger goals. Here's an example.

One of our night supervisors was going to college during the day. She was paying her way through school because she did not qualify for a scholarship. She was considering quitting her job so she could go to school full-time for as long as her money lasted. When we discussed her larger goal—to graduate from college—in the context of her smaller goal—to have a job in order to pay for school—she saw that she had to keep her job and continue going to school part-time. If she quit her job to attend college full-time, her money would soon be gone. Her job would be taken by someone else, and she might not have an opportunity to return to the same job with the same pay. If she went to work for someone else, she might not be allowed to work a schedule that would leave her time for school.

A review and evaluation session is not complete until employees have told you how you and the company are doing as employers. You need to ask them in what ways *you* could improve. Here's what we said: "Well, now I need to know how you think we're doing. Is there something you feel we should do that we aren't, or something we are doing that you wish we wouldn't do? We try to do the right thing. We just don't always know what it is. We need some feedback from you so we can improve, too."

If you have established a good rapport with your employees, and they are used to communicating with you and reporting mistakes, they will give you an honest evaluation and you will learn more about yourself and your company.

When you ask for constructive criticism, be sure you are prepared to deal with it. Remember, if a critical message comes from one source, the *messenger* is important. If a critical message comes from several sources, the *message* is important.

When I asked how I could do a better job, several managers and supervisors said I interrupted them when I burst into their offices with new ideas. They said I interrupted their train of thought. I thanked them and apologized for being insensitive and promised to do better.

It was very difficult for me to contain myself when I was enthused about an idea I wanted to share with them. I soon had to develop the habit of calling first or tapping on their door to see if they were busy before bursting in on them. I will always have a tendency to interrupt but knowing it helps to control it.

Reviews and evaluations of employees are good ways to motivate workers while you learn more about your employees. You will learn what they want from their jobs and what they want for themselves and their families. Your job is to help them achieve their goals with the work they do for your company.

As you learn more about them, you will also learn more about special talents they may have that you didn't know about. You can utilize those special talents for their benefit and yours.

OFFER FREELANCE WORK TO EMPLOYEES

Buying freelance work from employees can motivate workers and help you at the same time. Small companies often need additional help for a limited time or for a particular project. That's when you need to purchase freelance work from independent contractors. It's a common sense approach to a perennial problem, especially for small companies.

A couple of good reasons exist for doing this. First, you only purchase the work as needed, instead of making a long-term commitment by hiring another employee. Second, you only pay for the work after it is accepted, instead of paying while the person works on it. Traditionally, the independent contractor uses his or her own tools and supplies and works off the premises, saving you some wear and tear on your tools.

Purchasing freelance work from employees is a good way to utilize the talents of current workers who need moonlighting jobs and are looking for other opportunities to grow. It's also a good way to use the talents of former employees who have a good work record and need extra money. Offering freelance work to employees who are thinking of moonlighting, or are looking for other opportunities to use their skills, may be the deciding factor that keeps them on track. If they no longer work for your company, it may encourage them to return or at least keep the lines of communication open.

Consider the employees who need additional income and are tempted to take part-time work elsewhere. If your company purchases freelance work from them, both parties profit from it. The employees don't have to cope with two different work environments, and your company doesn't have to go outside to purchase work from strangers, hire additional help, or worry about the possibility of losing a good employee to the moonlighting job.

This is not to say that freelance work replaces overtime. If your company has overtime work available, and the additional work you want done is the same type of work that the employee does, then the additional work has to be billed as overtime wages. But if the additional work is different from what the employee normally does or is expected to do, and if you were going to purchase it outside the organization or have traditionally purchased it from independent contractors, then it can be purchased on the same basis from your employee.

We did it with several of our employees. We purchased freelance work from a packer who was taking woodworking courses at a vocational school after hours. He wanted to do carpentry work, and since we periodically used a carpenter to build things for us, we wanted to use him. We also purchased freelance work from one of our artists who was doing freelance work for an ad agency. She wanted extra jobs, and we periodically bought additional designs from outside freelance artists.

I checked with the wage and hour office first, explained what I wanted to do, and asked if it would be possible. I described their jobs and told them what we needed. They told me that the employees could submit their work on a freelance basis if the work did not involve the same duties they performed or were expected to perform as part of their jobs. In addition, the freelance work had to be done off the premises with their own tools and supplies, and we had to treat them as we treated other independent contractors submitting work.

We decided to invite all our employees to submit bids for work performed by independent contractors when needed. We were careful to treat all the bids—those of the independent contractors and those of our employees—in the same manner. Sometimes our employees were awarded the contracts; sometimes they weren't. We noticed an improvement in everyone's performance and more interest in their jobs.

If you need to purchase freelance work periodically, consider using the talents of your employees. It can pay dividends for both of you. But be careful and check with your local wage and hour office first, then follow their guidelines.

Your employees will appreciate your efforts to provide them with additional income and opportunities. And they will be more motivated to stay with you because they will know you recognize all their talents, not just those you see each day on the job. They will know you recognize them as individuals.

6.

How to Supervise the Right People

People want to work in a predictable environment. They want to know what is expected of them, because they want to do the right thing. But they don't always know what it is. Your job as a manager is to help them know. Good management is really using common sense to provide a predictable environment.

A good manager is analogous to a good teacher, which is analogous to a good parent. This is not in the hierarchical sense of an autocratic, dictatorial person, intimidating people with orders, but of an informed, educated person guiding people with wisdom.

Those who have information and insight that others don't possess have a responsibility to share it. Good managers have a commitment to help others grow by teaching them. Like teachers, they have to be dedicated, reliable, and dependable.

Supervising employees in your small business need not be difficult. Your training laid the foundation. Now you only need to accomplish these things: (1) be consistent, (2) be assertive, (3) communicate, (4) do it now, (5) follow through, and (6) discipline.

BE CONSISTENT

Be consistent implementing management policies and rules. When you are not, this causes several problems. First, you set a bad example your workers soon imitate. If you enforce a rule with one employee and not another, employees conclude, "If they don't have to keep that rule anymore, neither do I." If you enforce a rule with everyone some of the time but not all the time, employees decide, "If we didn't have to do it then, we don't have to do it now."

The second problem that develops is resentment for not enforcing the rule fairly or consistently. It is never a good idea to describe a policy or rule and say it's enforced and then not enforce it or enforce it haphazardly. If you enforce it with some people and not others, or on one occasion and not another, you create confusion among workers. You lose credibility, trust, and respect. If you do not intend to be consistent enforcing a policy or rule, don't adopt it.

In our small company we prided ourselves on being flexible, but there were two policies or rules that were "set in cement"—good attendance and good attitude. We enforced them consistently and fairly without vacillating, because we firmly believed they laid the foundation for implementing all the other rules. We knew if we consistently enforced our two most important rules, it would be much easier to enforce the others.

This was the most difficult thing we had to do, but it paid great dividends. It set the standard and gave us confidence. We considered them *major* policies. Other policies were important to us, but they were minor compared to those two. Our people knew it. I mentioned those policies in a previous chapter: good attendance and good attitude. We never hesitated enforcing those policies.

Minor policies may be altered or changed without ill effect because some policies need to change as your company grows and develops. But you need to be careful how you introduce changes or you will look inconsistent. You need to give some background explaining why you are changing the policy and how the change will improve your company in some way.

For example, if you discover your policy regarding working hours is not convenient for some of your people, you need to consider changing it. Maybe you need more than one shift, or you need to provide a rotating shift. Whatever you and your people decide is best, do it, but in an organized, structured manner so your people know the change was carefully thought out before you set it in motion.

Handling Worker Suggestions

Worker suggestions or needs may bring about a change in policy or may be the impetus for the change. If you handle it correctly, and their actions are directed through proper channels, the policy change will be the result of cooperative behavior—not a weakening of wills, or a giving-in to worker pressure.

If you discover any minor policy or rule that needs to be changed, change it, but in an organized manner. If your company is flexible, and it should be if you intend to grow and improve, you need to provide for change. We gave bonuses to people who discovered better ways of doing things. Any change that comes about as a result of people working through recognized channels is not destructive.

Changes that occur when you are not consistent are destructive, because what *you* do automatically teaches others what to do. Their attitude, behavior, and overall performance are internalized during their training and reinforced daily in your department. If they observe you saying one thing and doing another; promising to take action, then forgetting, you have taught them two things: to be inconsistent and to procrastinate. Conversely, if you do what you say and keep your promises, you set a good example and teach workers two good work habits: to be consistent and to follow through.

BE ASSERTIVE

Be assertive and you will have less difficulty enforcing policies consistently. Most of us hesitate to be assertive in the following situations: when we have to challenge aggressive or belligerent people; when we have to confront coworkers with their mistakes; and when we have to oppose the actions of others.

There are reasons managers aren't assertive in these situations: they may be intimidated by the person they have to confront; they may not like giving facts they fear will hurt people's feelings; or they may feel they don't have the authority to act. Weak managers give excuses for not being assertive: they thought the problem would resolve itself; they thought the problem wouldn't get any worse; or they thought someone else would take care of the problem.

The first step to becoming assertive is to admit that no problem will resolve itself; a problem will always get worse; and no one will take care of a problem for you. If you can accept those facts and that it is your responsibility to solve problems, half the battle is won.

The second step is to become confident. If you are confident, you have no difficulty being assertive and facing daily problems. How do you become confident? What does it mean? It means to be assured, secure, certain, and positive. The opposite meaning is to be insecure or dubious. You can't feel insecure and dubious if you know your job, trust your company, and believe in its policies. Faith in yourself and the company provides you with everything you need to be confident.

You can learn to become assertive a little at a time. Establish one or two policies you feel provide a foundation for the others, and be assertive with those two policies. Whatever you select, make those the pivotal ones that support your actions for maintaining the others. If you effectively maintain just one or two policies, it will give you the confidence to be assertive supporting the others. The reason is, you are establishing an assertive habit by being consistent with just one or two policies.

Watching others who are assertive is another way to acquire the habit. We made a point of having supervisors observe experienced managers in disciplinary sessions before they tried handling such sessions themselves. The managers always wrote training reports describing the results. (See Figure 8.)

COMMUNICATE

Communicate well and your management duties will be simplified. One of your primary duties as a manager is to establish a good relationship with your workers, one that requires mutual trust. You establish mutual trust when you satisfy workers' needs: to feel secure; to feel they belong; and to feel they can grow in the job. All this involves self-esteem. Workers must feel good about themselves and what they are doing. Anything that undermines their self-esteem weakens mutual trust. And all this hinges on good communication.

Workers don't feel good about themselves when they make mistakes. Your job is to help prevent mistakes. There are two basic reasons people make mistakes: lack of attention when instructions are given, or when carrying them out; and lack of understanding, due to incorrect or incomplete information. Both involve poor communication.

Lack of Attention

Let's discuss lack of attention first. Most people have short attention spans. They listen and absorb the first bit of information they receive. If the original bit is changed, the listener has a tendency not to hear it. Their attention has shifted, looking for new information. That's why, for example, when you give a food order to a waiter and change part of the order, he brings you the wrong order. The

The same phenomenon occurs in other work-related tasks. If you change segments of your instructions while giving them, chances are, the worker will ignore the changes. Therefore, try not to change bits of information when giving instructions. Know what you are going to say. Rehearse it if you have to, but strive to state it correctly the first time—without changes.

Lack of attention is not the only reason people make mistakes. If workers are not given correct or complete information in a way they understand, they will be more likely to make a mistake. Therefore, it is a good idea to examine what you want to say and make certain you say it in a way your listener understands. If you have to use simpler terminology, analogies, or comparisons to get your message across, do so. If you need to give written instructions, do so.

Ensuring Your Instructions are Understood

To further ensure your instructions are understood, restate them, emphasizing the essentials. Then have the listener repeat the instructions in his own words.

When I began training supervisors to do this, they thought it was unnecessary until they witnessed the results. I had them observe me giving a worker instructions to complete three tasks. I asked the worker to repeat the instructions before carrying them out. When the worker repeated them, part of the instructions was missing.

A final word of caution. Always give instructions directly to the person who is to carry out the task. If the instructions are passed from one person to another, there is a greater chance a mistake will be made. Misinformation and misunderstandings occur most often when instructions are passed from one person to another. Accompany verbal instructions with written instructions, so you have a record of your communication.

To avoid mistakes in communication: be sure you know what you want to say; give correct and complete information without changing it; say it in a way listeners will understand; have the listeners repeat it in their own words; and include written instructions when you can. If the listeners still make mistakes, probe deeper to uncover reasons for their lack of attention.

Communication involves more than giving instructions. It means listening, being alert, being aware of your surroundings, and

Figure 8
TRAINING THE PLANT MANAGER

Attached is a report from my backup on how she handled a people problem. Over the past year since she was promoted to plant manager I have been in on all people situations with her. First with me handling the problem and her listening, and then with her handling the problem and me listening. After this we went through the procedure of having her handle the problem by herself with me observing from another office.

When she brought me the situation she describes on the attached sheet, I felt she should handle this one by herself and report back to me. I discussed it with her and she felt very confident in doing it. We didn't feel it was a case where the person would give her any problem, and it wasn't a strict disciplinary act. We followed our normal procedure and rehearsed what she would say, and she handled it by herself with her assistant observing.

I talked with my backup afterward, and she felt very good about how it went with no problem. I will always continue to be in on people situations because I want to be, but I want her to start handling some minor ones on her own. She needs to build some self-confidence.

keeping an open mind. When any worker mentions a problem, it's important for a supervisor to learn the reasons for the problem, so it can be solved. Supervisors in our small company daily discussed problems with their plant manager. This passing of information along the lines was important because sharing it among themselves and with the plant manager often prevented misinformation from spreading. Misinformation is the most destructive element in a workplace and is always the result of poor communication. Supervisors have a never-ending job keeping misinformation to a minimum. If you listen with an open mind and take action by communicating with workers and other managers, you will limit misinformation.

DO IT NOW

Do it now, and you will limit management problems. As a manager, you set the standard in your department. If your standard is high, your department's will be, too. One of the factors contributing to a high standard is prompt action. If you have the habit of acting promptly, so will your workers.

If you see workers who are making mistakes or aren't interested in their jobs, take action now. Suggest ways to help them. Don't wait. The longer you wait, the greater the chances their mistakes will become habits. Some psychology books say people learn faster when you praise their good work and ignore their bad work. I disagree. Everyone learns faster, and with less frustration, if they are guided along the way and kept informed of their progress.

When managers procrastinate, they only postpone the inevitable. Problems get worse, and sometimes new problems develop that could have been avoided if prompt action had been taken. In some cases, indecision is the reason managers put things off until later.

If you need to make a tough decision, do it now. The longer you put it off, the worse it gets. Since problems with people can quickly escalate out of control, those are the ones that need the most attention. If you need to discipline a person, don't wait three or four days. Workers have a right to know how they are doing now.

It doesn't matter whether you are giving constructive criticism or praise—do it now. If you are pleased with the way employees are performing, and want them to continue, compliment them: "You're doing a good job. You really catch on fast." They will work with more confidence and enthusiasm, and they will be motivated to learn.

If the employees are not doing a good job, it's just as important to take action promptly. Say, "I think maybe we have a little problem here. I notice you don't appear to be interested. Did we give you the proper instructions?" Wait for a reply and discuss it with them. If the instructions were sufficient then ask, "Does the new job interest you?" Find out, but do it now. The longer you wait, the longer they will be working, thinking they are doing okay or that they can get by with little effort. If you want to work with a high quality standard, you are teaching them just the opposite by letting them continue with a standard you don't want.

Whenever you see employees doing something that could lead to problems later, take action now to point it out before it becomes a problem. It may seem as though you are overreacting, but it's necessary to respond quickly to potential problems. Our managers were especially sensitive to people's feelings. (See Figure 9.)

If you are compiling a report that others rely on for information—do it now. If you wait, you may disrupt their schedule or they may miss a deadline. If you are writing a training report, doing a job evaluation, or documenting a disciplinary action—do it now. You may forget small details that are relevant.

Good managers carry paper and pencils so they can take notes. That's because they have the "do it now" habit. They know if they don't jot down facts or impressions now, they might forget them later. All good managers should have the same "do it now" habit. If you don't, start now to develop it.

FOLLOW THROUGH

Follow through and you will avoid most problems. You will find you have to train your managers to follow through with tasks you assign them and with tasks they assign themselves and others. After you have trained your own staff to follow through for your company, you will find they also have to follow through for other companies that don't train their staffs to follow through.

When you follow through, you set the standard. When you don't follow through, you let others set the standard. When vendors promise to deliver an order—and don't—when service companies say they will stop by—and don't—when customers say they will call

---

Figure 9
LUNCHROOM REMINDER

While handing out paychecks January 3rd with each person, the plant manager and I took the opportunity to go over lunchroom policies again. The reason is some of the girls brought snacks and extra food for the New Year's holiday. The lunchroom was left a mess at the end of the day when they left and also, again everyone was not invited in on the little lunchtime activity.

We explained to everyone that, first of all, if in the future they want to do something like that for the holidays, the plant manager and I must be aware of it. Second, someone must be in charge of cleaning up at the end of the day after everyone leaves. Third, everyone must be involved in it.

We explained why we feel that everyone should be involved in all the activities that go on at work. If it's something that's done strictly after work we do not have anything to do with it, but if they are taking up the lunchroom with extra food, that is involving everyone and they must have the courtesy to give everyone the opportunity to participate.

A lot of the girls seemed to readily know what we were saying and definitely agreed with this, as it is not fair not to involve everyone. We explained how the girls who work in the front office and the upstairs office are the same as us in the back, and there is be no separation between any of the departments. That is the way everything should be handled.

They all agreed with this. I don't think we'll have future problems.

back—and don't—you and your managers will have to follow through for them. Otherwise, their standard will become your standard.

In our company we were training a supervisor who wasn't moving ahead as fast as he wanted. We pointed to his lack of follow-through. For example, if a delivery was not on time, he waited for the plant manager to tell him to call and inquire about it. If people promised to call back and didn't, he never followed through by calling them back. When he called for repairs and the service company told him to wait for their call, he never asked them when they would call. Instead, he waited and waited. After we showed him how his lack of follow-through permitted others to set their low standard for him and his department, he began to improve—and to follow through.

Good managers assign duties and expect results; they guarantee those results by following through. They set a deadline and ask for progress reports. They send memos or informally stop by to see how things are going. If a report isn't on time, they ask why. If a deadline is missed, they show concern and probe deeper for underlying causes. They question their own instructions. Were they clear? Did the people understand what the manager wanted? These things all represent follow-through.

One effective way to get people to follow through is to work with a sense of urgency. When you call for information or service and are told, "We'll get back to you," ask "When?" Make them set a time. Tell them if they don't call by a certain time, you will call them again. Keep your word and call them again.

When a delivery is scheduled, set a definite time, and make arrangements for someone to sign for the package. If it doesn't arrive on time, call and keep calling until the item is delivered. Report the slow delivery to the manager of the company. Next time they will give you better service.

Following through on other companies is time consuming, but it will pay off with better service. After working with some companies, you will notice their performance will improve. They may not follow through with other companies, but they will follow through with yours, because they know you expect it. They know you maintain high standards and you won't let them or other companies compromise those standards. (See Figures 10 and 11.)

When you assign duties to employees, be specific with directions, explanations, and deadlines. Then follow through by checking on them next time you are in the department. They will know you haven't forgotten. If the assignment extends over a period of time, make arrangements for them to give you a report on how things are progressing. That's follow-through.

DISCIPLINE

Discipline is the most difficult part of managing. It requires using other management skills, such as consistency, assertiveness, communication, promptness, and follow-through. If you are a good manager and you have been firm in your commitment to company policies, fair in implementing those policies, courteous with employees, prompt in your actions, and have followed through by keeping your word, you will find disciplinary action is easier.

Disciplinary action implies confrontation. Any important confrontation should be planned in advance. To use an analogy, no general goes into battle without first studying the lay of the land from all angles. The general plans what is to be done, who is going to do it, how, and when, and he rehearses it in his mind. He knows what is going to happen before he begins. Then after the confrontation, he reviews what occurred to see what could have been done better. He wants every battle to be a learning experience.

A Four-Step Process

Disciplinary confrontations with employees should be engaged in the same manner. We used a four-step process. You may want to adopt it. When a supervisor brings a problem to your attention or to your plant manager's attention, the first step is to discuss the problem in detail. Make sure everyone connected with the problem has an opportunity to tell what they know about it. The supervisor and the other manager decide the best way to handle the problem.

The second step is to rehearse what the manager is going to say. In most cases, the supervisor does the talking, so it is that person who rehearses what is to be said. The best way to rehearse is to role play and use notes. Have the supervisor say what is actually going to be

Figure 10
SUPERVISOR MEETING SITUATION REPORTS

Situation: As plant manager, I checked three-ounce bottles of liquid gold that had just been delivered and found that some were only partially filled yet all were priced the same. I poured the gold from the three-ounce bottles into one-ounce bottles and found that some of the three-ounce bottles had as little as 2/3 the amount of gold as other bottles. The price of gold was currently at $400 per ounce. This meant that some bottles varied in cost as much as one ounce, or $400.

Solution: I called the gold supplier and told them about it. I asked them to come and check the other half-full bottles with me if necessary. I insisted they credit the company account for the difference.

> Common Sense tells you to report a defective or improper shipment immediately before it is used, so that you have proof of your claim.

Situation: As warehouse supervisor, I placed an order with a vendor for supplies needed in my department. When the order arrived, it was a larger quantity than I ordered.

Solution: I contacted the vendor and told them I received more than I ordered, and I had a copy of the original purchase order, and I was returning the unwanted portion C.O.D. and the payment of the bill would reflect the returns. I notified the accounting department that the bill should not be paid in full but in the amount I specified.

> Common Sense tells you that you shouldn't pay for what you don't want. It is a policy of some vendors to overship on orders hoping you will pay for them.

Situation: As supervisor of the kiln department, I had to call a repairman. He said he would be at the plant at a certain time but he never came.

Solution: I called him back to find out why he didn't arrive and how soon he could come.

> Common Sense tells you to take action immediately when people don't show up. Let them know you expect them.

Figure 11
SUPERVISOR MEETING SITUATION
REPORTS FROM V.P.

UPS makes a pickup at our company once a day. The shipping clerk brought to my attention that they were coming too early in the afternoon, which meant a lot of priority packages couldn't go. So we called the area office and talked to the manager and arranged to have a later pickup (not before 4:00). It worked out fine for approximately one month.

One day the shipping clerk came to me and said there was a new driver, and he had come earlier than he was supposed to. She asked him if he could not wait for five minutes so she could stamp a couple of boxes that were priority. He said no. I went back and explained to him that we arranged with the area office to have a later pickup because of this very problem. He became VERY rude and said, "I don't know how you arranged that one Sweetie, but I'm the temporary driver this week and I'm not waiting even five minutes."

It was obvious that there was no communicating with this rude man, so I turned around and went directly to my office. I called the area office and talked to the manager. I explained what had just happened. He apologized and sent another driver out to pick up our packages that didn't get shipped. I asked accounting to give me a total of the dollar amount of business we did with UPS in the past year. I then wrote a letter to the head of personnel in Pittsburgh with a copy to the area manager. The result was a visit from the rude driver and his manager to apologize to me in person.

Common Sense tells you that if a person servicing the company in any way treats you or one of your people improperly, you should report this to the company's manager. They will appreciate your taking the time to bring this to their attention.

The service man from the electric company bothered Mr. Tway again about the kilns when we're the ones who know about them. It wastes everyone's time when they don't talk with us because we are girls.

Mr. Tway called the electric company and told the owner that he is in sales and doesn't know the kilns, and if the repairmen continued bothering him and not talking with the girls at the kiln who work on them we would change service companies.

Common Sense tells you to go to the top when you have tried working with the other people from the company.

said while you, or the other manager, say what you think the employee will say. You will be pleasantly surprised at how successful disciplinary sessions will be when you plan ahead, develop a script, and role play ahead of time.

The third step is to call the employee to the office with the supervisor and other manager and discuss the problem, using the conversation the supervisor has rehearsed. Justify using your notes by saying, "I made some notes because I don't want to forget anything." Conclude your disciplinary session by writing a dated memo that the employee signs. You can say, "I don't want us to forget we had this talk, so I'm making a note of it and need all of us to sign it." Never take any disciplinary action without a witness and a written, dated memo to document it.

The fourth step is to examine the conversation that just took place—after the employee leaves the room. This is an important part of the process because it is through self-examination that man-agers improve their performance. After the confrontation, the managers who were present should go over what occurred and review what was said, how it was said, and how it could have been done better.

Every confrontation should be a learning experience. It will be, if you take the time to review it immediately after it occurred. I know it's difficult to do because you are sick of it by then, but it is necessary if you and the other participants are going to learn from it. You have an opportunity to make suggestions for improving next time. If you and the other managers write a short, descriptive report of the session and your opinions of it, you will have an additional record for the employee's file and a record of your performances as managers.

If the action is a termination, do it briefly, objectively backing up your action with documentation. If it is disciplinary action and the person is remaining on the job, the latter part of the confrontation should be positive, pointing toward improvement.

Setting a Standard

We encountered four basic kinds of disciplinary meetings. The first kind was not serious enough to consider drastic action or termination. This type requires setting the standard so the employee knows you are consistent and that you follow through on policies. The employee may have a poor attendance record or act as if in working for you he is doing you a favor. The worker may have complained to coworkers about long hours, the work load, or the workplace in general. It is clear the employee has broken an important company policy, either with poor attendance or poor attitude by complaining to coworkers, instead of bringing problems to the supervisor. You need to be patient and not overreact because the individual may be a good employee who has acquired a bad habit in another workplace where the standards were lower. Or the individual may be a bad employee you will have to terminate sooner or later. Whichever type he or she is, the employee is testing you—perhaps unconsciously—but still testing you. Don't fail the test. When this occurs, meet the challenge immediately and call the bluff. If you pass this first test you won't have any more trouble—if the person is a good employee. The number of times you have to talk with the individual in this manner indicates how good that employee is. We always gave two written warnings before termination. You need to be firm—not mean or angry or threatening—just firm, friendly, and businesslike.

Call the employee in for a private conversation. Begin by saying, "I understand you ..." and show the attendance record if that is the problem. If attitude is the problem, repeat the complaints made to coworkers and explain why they should have been taken to the supervisor. Try to find out what is bothering the employee and try to arrive at a viable solution if the complaint is legitimate.

Get a commitment for improvement. This puts the responsibility on the employee. If you can't get a commitment, say, "I have to ask you if you want to continue working here." Don't say anything else! Be silent. Let the silence work for you. Sit and look at the person. In most cases, you will get a response. If you don't, say, "I feel you may want to think about it. So I'll talk with you later today." Set a definite time for later that day or after work. Always conclude with, "We'd like to have you with our company but only if you're completely sold on us and have good attendance and a good attitude."

Problem on the Job

The second type of disciplinary meeting is one in which employees haven't done what you have asked them to do as a necessary part of their job. The problem could involve quality, production, or some other aspect you consider important. After you call the employee in for a private meeting, show him your records of his work and point out in what ways he has not met the minimum standard. Be specific! This is why it is so necessary to keep accurate records.

After going over the facts, say, "Can you think of a legitimate reason why we should have this problem?" If he gives excuses, remind him that he agreed at the time of the assignment that it wasn't a problem. If there is a legitimate reason for the problem, say, "I'm aware of problems that develop like this; however, your job is to let me know when you can't follow through on assignments so I can make alternate plans."

Have him go back and immediately complete the assignment, even though it may be past due and out of date. Also make him write a memo stating that it will be late and citing the reason. This teaches him that he cannot get out of an assignment. Leave the meeting with the same positive message: "We want you to be a part of our team but that means responding like other team members: getting reports in, following through on assignments, and reporting back when you can't complete assignments or when assignments will be late."

Remind employees that getting things done, following through on assignments, and communicating by memos are ways you evaluate employees for pay raises and promotions. Remind them that you have to document situations like this one. When you have finished, don't continue talking. Get their commitment to correct the situation and let them go.

Warning of Termination

The third type of confrontation is one in which there is reason to believe the employee must either change or face termination. The best approach is to state the facts and support those facts with your records. Use notes to ensure you won't misstate something. Say, "I've made notes so I would be sure not to omit important points." After stating the facts, add, "At this point (use his or her name), I have to ask if you really want to continue with us." Be silent! When the employee expresses a desire to continue, give specific guidelines the person must follow, a probation period, and a date when you will make your final decision about the individual's progress.

Termination

The fourth type of confrontation is a termination. The termination can be due to lack of production, lack of ability to perform the job, deliberate carelessness, or unacceptable performance for reasons within the employee's control. Always schedule a termination session for the end of the week or the end of the day if you can. It is less disruptive to the other employees. (See Figure 12.)

State the facts and back them with records, showing the employee in what ways he did not meet company standards. If you are using two written warnings before termination, be sure you show those. Conclude with: "You can see that you have not met our minimum standards. Therefore, I have no recourse but to let you go. I've had our bookkeeper make out your check." Hand him the check. Be silent! If he doesn't move toward the door, get up and open the door, and see him out.

The more you say during a disciplinary confrontation, the more misunderstandings can occur. Remember the three B's: be bright, be brief, and be gone. With every disciplinary encounter, have a witness, document what you do, and have the employee sign the documentation with the date. Even for minor disciplinary sessions, I said something like this: "I get busy, and I know you do too, so we might forget we had this talk. To jog our memory, we both need a reminder." Show him the documentation and have him initial it.

Before every encounter, go over the four-step procedure: get the facts and decide what you are going to do; rehearse what you are going to do; do it; afterward, review what you did to see how you could improve it. Make every disciplinary session a learning session. You won't dread them so much. We made many of those encounters teaching sessions. (See Figure 13.)

When Employees Quit

Before leaving the subject of the four-step procedure used in disciplinary sessions, I want to mention another instance when a variation of it can be used—when employees quit. You already know why the people you terminated are leaving, and you probably know how they feel about your company. But what about those other people who, for one reason or another, quit their jobs and move on?

Figure 12
TERMINATION REPORT ON TRAINEE

We called the trainee in to terminate her. We reminded her that we had talked to her on two separate occasions about her attitude. The first time, on September 20th, she was told that we did not want to have to say this again to her. The second time, on October 8th, was her last and final warning that if we ever had any problem we would have to terminate her.

Since that time, we have had numerous complaints from several different people in the studio about her. She gets mad when the inspector gives her back plates that are bad. She gets mad if the person beside her won't help her with her plates. She constantly complains about the project she is on. She distracts the people she sits beside and brings them down at the same time. These are all complaints that we have had from the girls who work with her in the studio. For these reasons, we called her in and terminated her because she had two previous warnings about her attitude.

Figure 13
TEACHING SUPERVISOR
TO DISCIPLINE REPORT

On Friday we had to talk with an employee about her attendance. I went over with my trainee the correct procedure as a manager in handling a disciplinary situation. I told her the steps were: 1. Discuss all the details involved. 2. Rehearse what to say and who will say it. 3. Actually talk to the person. 4. Discuss afterward how we felt it went, what was the person's reaction, and how we could have done it better for the next time.

This is what the trainee and I did. I told her that I would do the talking to the employee since I talked to her before about this same problem and also because in training she will be listening to me a few times before she does the talking while I listen. The trainee understood all this.

She is a strong person and I think she will do well when it is her turn to handle something with me there observing. She had no questions. She asked me if it would be wrong for the person who is listening to add something during the session. I told her yes and no. If it was something I forgot that we rehearsed, she could add it. But if it was something she just thought of, she shouldn't add it. If it was that important, we should have discussed it ahead of time. Adding it now might confuse things. I also told the trainee we always write up every incident for the file. We both wrote it up and I put the reports in the trainee's file.

Wouldn't you like to know how they would evaluate your company? Even if you do all the right things, you will still have people leave your company. When this happened in our company, we always made a point of having a friendly visit with the employee before she left. We wished her well and asked her a couple of questions.

You may want to adopt this procedure. It has some of the characteristics of the disciplinary method. And like that method, it's a good idea to have another manager with you. Your objective is to get an honest evaluation of your company and your employees from someone who is leaving. Decide what you want to know, rehearse how you are going to say it, then have your visit and afterward discuss your findings with the other manager who sat in on the session. Then review all this with your other managers and supervisors so you will all benefit from it.

Here are a couple of the comments and questions we included. "We enjoyed working with you and hope you find what you want in your next job. Do you remember our first interview when we asked about your strengths and weaknesses?" She will say yes. "We know we have them too. I'd like to know what you think our company's strengths and weaknesses are." At this point don't hurry her. Let her talk and probe different areas you think need to be explored. You will learn a great deal from these final sessions if you approach them in the right way with the right attitude.

Part of your turnover rate will be determined by the characteristics of your work force. For example, almost all our employees were young women whose lives were in transition. They were either getting married, having babies, leaving their husbands, or moving away with them. A few were preparing for college or attending school part-time. We periodically lost key people who went away to college or moved away with their husbands. We lost other key people for short periods when they had babies.

Despite these normal causes for a high turnover rate, during the fourteen years we owned our company, we retained more than a third of our original work force. They became our key people, our supervisors and managers. You can view that figure optimistically, which we did. Or you can view it pessimistically—losing two-thirds of the people who were hired and trained. On the surface it appears costly, but we made up for it in other ways.

The people we did retain were exemplary, as evidenced by our personnel records: 2% sick leave, 1% tardiness, and under 2% absentee rate. Our unemployment and worker's compensation rates were actually lower than the minimum used by the state at that time. That makes up for the cost of the high turnover and low hiring rate—especially given the added pleasure of working with good people.

Unemployment and Worker's Compensation Hearings

A final use of the disciplinary method is to prepare for an unemployment or worker's compensation hearing. The closer you come to maintaining the right relationship with employees, being assertive and consistent and documenting, the less trouble you will have defending your actions. You can do everything right to the best of your ability and still have unemployment claims against you. It is your responsibility to prove your innocence.

The unemployment office exists to help both employers and employees. I discuss this relationship in the final chapter under the section dealing with your image in the community. Here, however, I want to focus on the best method to use when you must appear at an unemployment hearing or an appeal.

The basic procedures are the same as those for disciplinary action. Get all the facts and all the documents, including those you will have from the unemployment office, and review them in detail. Know what it is you are defending. Be sure you have all the documents you need, including the time cards. In twelve years, we lost only a handful of cases. One of them was the very first case, at which time I didn't know we were responsible for bringing the employee's time cards to the hearing. I learned the hard way.

Once you know what you need to say, rehearse it in detail. Role play, taking the part of the examiner, the employee, and yourselves. You must have every person testify who can in any way contribute firsthand knowledge of the situation being reviewed. You cannot rely on hearsay. Only first person testimony is admissible.

If you are going to serve as your own attorney, you will have an opportunity to cross-examine employees after they have testified and after you have testified. We only had an attorney one time and lost the case. We decided we would do better ourselves if we prepared ahead of time and knew exactly what to say and what not to say.

It is important that you be relaxed, and you will be if you are thoroughly prepared. Since I had taught body language at an earlier time, I made a point of training the supervisors to project a favorable image. We sat up straight, kept our hands on the table, and made sure to look the examiner in the eye when talking with her or him. We did not get angry or appear flustered by talking too fast or too loud. We also did not mumble or whisper. We spoke distinctly and with confidence because we knew we were right.

When you go to any hearing at which you have to testify, always look your questioners in the eye. If you have a problem doing this, look at a spot between their eyes. It gives the appearance that you are looking at them and will cause you less difficulty.

After you leave the hearing, remember to complete the four-step procedure with a review. You want to talk it over with all the participants who testified for you. Then you and the manager or supervisor who attended the hearing will want to discuss it further. You can use your next supervisors' meeting to share your experiences as a learning session for the others.

If you have any worker's compensation hearings, you can use the same four-step procedure. We only had one unjust claim against us, and after attending two hearings our insurance agents told us to let them handle it because of the amount of time we wasted showing up for hearings when the claimant never showed up.

The four-step procedure we used for disciplinary action is a good one. You can use it for any session that involves a confrontation you find intimidating. Knowing what you want, planning ahead, practicing, then doing it with confidence and following up with an evaluation and documentation will get you through it. And what is more important, you will learn from it.

7.

How to Develop the Right People

There are two kinds of manager—those who manage and develop managers and those who manage but don't develop managers. Some people are natural developers; others are managers but non-developers. Both are productive and necessary for your business.

Let's compare their differences. A developer has the capacity to work with subordinates in detailed, repetitive situations. A non-developer either isn't interested or doesn't have the patience. The developer enjoys going through the basics, analyzing and redefining tasks. The non-developer prefers working on a level that takes those basics for granted. The developer enjoys going to the valleys to climb the mountain again and again with different trainees. The non-developer has climbed the mountain once and prefers not to do it again—with anyone. The developer enjoys watching others learn to perform a task. The non-developer enjoys knowing the task is completed, not *how* it was completed.

Developing managers for your small business is a challenge. You will succeed if you do several things: (1) teach, (2) promote, (3) admit mistakes, (4) meet frequently, (5) structure, and (6) let go.

TEACH

Teach. If you are going to develop people, one of the benefits you will derive from teaching is learning. The best way to learn more about something is to teach it. You will find new ways of expressing yourself and discover different aspects of a subject you thought you knew. Whenever you work with people, you benefit because you share what you know with others, and in the process you acquire something from them.

You may have neglected to tell your people something because it's not meaningful to you, but you discover it is to them. Suddenly, it becomes meaningful to you too because you have another perspective. As a good developer, you include this new insight in your future training procedures. That's an important part of your job as a manager—to acquire new knowledge and pass it on.

Maybe you try to teach something that's not significant to those being taught because they don't have your background and experience. It becomes necessary for you to discover a way to present it so they can appreciate it too. This process of discovery for them results in discovery for you and becomes another training tool for you to use with others.

As you teach, you will enjoy seeing new managers grow and develop, learning to do things you have taught them and going beyond what you have taught them. You will enjoy watching new managers discover new ways of doing what you do, expressing themselves differently to achieve the same thing, combining their style with yours to create a better way. The finest tribute to a teacher is cultivating a student who surpasses the teacher. As a developer of people, keep working toward this goal and you will be richly rewarded. If it is true parents achieve immortality through their progeny, it is even more true that teachers achieve immortality through their students. If you develop people to become managers, you leave an indelible mark on the future of your company and your industry. This is a heady thought and a challenge, but it carries a weighty responsibility.

Provide an Environment Conducive to Learning

Your major goal is to help people learn to acquire new skills, see things from a different perspective, listen more intently, and say things in a new way. Provide an environment that is conducive to learning—they will see opportunities where they never saw them before. Teach them to become more aware of their surroundings and what goes on around them—they will solve problems more easily.

Take the time to explain why and how things are done even if you think it may be unnecessary. If you do this, trainees will acquire all the skills they need to help others. Part of those skills include explaining "how" and "why." Your trainees will realize they are responsible for others as well as themselves and develop your training habits.

Use Every Opportunity to Teach

One of those training habits is to utilize every opportunity to teach. When any management situation occurs that might provide an example for your trainees, call them in to witness it with you. It will teach them to share your concern and learn from your behavior. Everything they see you do as a manager affects what they do and how they do it. Your job as a developer is to teach good followers to become good leaders. Your trainees know how to follow your plans. Your job now is to teach them how to make their own plans. You need to teach them to plan ahead, to know where to go, and to lead others. In the process, they must learn how to look at a job, analyze it, classify it, and define it for others.

As a developer, you must be friendly but know the difference between being friendly and being a friend. You can't be a buddy and a boss. Like all good managers, you need to be fair and firm but know the difference between being firm and being autocratic. If you are firm and consistent, you foster security and a learning environment. If you are autocratic, you generate fear and thwart any chance for learning.

Like all good managers, you need to follow through, check things out, and probe deeper. Do not leave to chance any minor opportunity to point out something that might help trainees later. You need consistently to show them things they might not have noticed.

As a developer, you need to be sensitive to the feelings of others and treat your trainees the way you would want to be treated. Always put yourself in their place. Ask yourself how you would feel under the same circumstances. Try to see things from their point of view before you take action.

Find New Perspectives

You need to create new ways to present information so that others understand. Always look ahead to see what things need to be taught. When you're not sure, ask your trainees. They'll tell you. Then plan ways for them to secure the information or skills they feel they lack. Use analogies to make your points.

Here is an analogy to illustrate how to see things from a different perspective. Holding an object up between you and your trainees, ask them to describe it from their side. Then you describe the same object from your side. Turn it around and go through the same procedure. Make the point with them: what you describe is what you see and what you see is limited to your point of view. Make another point: a manager's job is to turn things around so they can see things from all points of view. This may be a new way of thinking for them.

As a developer, know when to pull back, when to provide a helpful hint and when to let the trainee give advice, when to probe with questions and when to listen, when to motivate the trainee with encouragement and when to be silent so a deeper feeling can emerge if you sense the need. (See Figure 14.)

Look for underlying messages when trainees complain. Realize that confusion and bewilderment are a natural part of the learning process, especially when it involves managing. Try to safeguard against discouragement and frustration by providing a structured program that includes guidelines along the way.

A Training Program

A manager's training program needs to be tightly structured at the beginning, proceeding step by step and becoming less structured as trainees gain confidence. Later, they will be able to rely on outlines and checklists until finally they need to give you only periodic reports.

As you develop trainees into managers, you need to instill confidence in them. Give them an honest appraisal of their strengths and weaknesses as you work with them. Rely on their strengths and accept their weaknesses and they won't disappoint you. Training new managers will be the most rewarding thing you do for yourself and your company.

PROMOTE

Promote with care. One of the dangers you face when you develop people is promoting too fast. The worker who is prematurely promoted may rise to the occasion and successfully meet the challenges of the new job, or sink to oblivion by never risking another

Figure 14
TRAINING REPORT ON SALES SERVICE PERSON

A situation came up in the sales meeting the other day that required me to talk afterwards to one of our sales service people who is learning to train her backup. It involved knowing when to pull back when you are training a new person. I had specifically asked that sales service person's trainee a question about something the trainee was doing with an account, and the sales service trainer answered the question before her trainee had a chance to. I later told the trainer that I am sure I didn't need to tell her that the trainee will not learn if the trainer answers questions for her.

I told the trainer that I knew the answer to the question but I wanted to see if the trainee knew the answer, and that was the reason I was asking it. When the trainer answered it for the trainee, it didn't help the trainee learn at all. The sales service trainer understood this right away.

This is not a big problem with her when she trains people, but I wanted to mention it to her so she would be aware of it and it didn't become a problem. Since the time I talked to her about it I have noticed if someone asks her trainee something in a meeting, the trainer will sometimes begin to answer and then put her hand over her mouth and say, "I'm sorry, you go ahead." It's a habit she is aware of now and is working on.

promotion or by quitting. It is necessary to find ways to prevent failures; or if a failure occurs, to limit it to a temporary setback.

Offer Options

There are several steps you can take to prevent failures. The first is to give trainees the option of returning to their former job if the new one doesn't work out. Most people, even successful ones, fear failure. Part of that fear is fear of losing something that is familiar. Even though an employee's current job has its problems, she is confident she can handle them because she has done so in the past. She is comfortable simply because she knows the nature of familiar problems and has survived them.

New situations represent the unknown, and people fear the unknown. It will help if you assure your trainees they can have their old job back if they don't like the new one. A second step is to announce the promotion in such a way that the person's ego is protected. If the general announcement is postponed until after she has been trained and is functioning in the new position for a while, it takes some of the pressure off. If the trainee has second thoughts about remaining in the new job, she can say so because she doesn't feel "locked in" to save face.

If the person works out in the new position, there will be plenty of time to make the formal announcement, which can come in two stages. The first stage can be phrased in such a way that you commend the person for her help and the job she's been doing, and that you've asked her to stay on a while to see whether she likes it. Later, you can announce that she's been performing the task successfully for a period of time, and you feel she deserves the promotion to go along with the job.

If you promote a worker to supervisor and she doesn't feel qualified, let her try the position unannounced for a period of time as a "fill-in" on a temporary basis, without a formal announcement. When coworkers ask about the change, you can say the person is helping out for now by filling in while you look for a supervisor.

Later, after the trainee has successfully been handling the job and feels she likes it and is secure, you can make a formal announcement."Diane has been helping out as a supervisor for some time now and has done such a good job we have asked her to continue in that capacity. She has agreed and we're delighted."

You may find you have to make a formal announcement at the time you promote someone because the job has been vacant for a while. Everyone knows you're looking for a supervisor. You can announce it in a way that protects the worker and gives him the opportunity to change his mind without embarrassment. You can say, "Jim has agreed to try the job as supervisor to help us out for now. He likes his old job so much, he is hesitant to leave it permanently. But he has agreed to give this job a try, just to help us while we continue to look for someone. If Jim really likes it, he has first shot at it. But if he still prefers his old job he can have it. In the meantime, we've promised Jim we will still be looking."

After the trainee is successfully working in the job, the manager can announce, "Jim likes the challenge of the new job so much, he has decided to keep it. Congratulations, Jim."

Sometimes a worker has all the qualities and experience to be a manager but refuses to try. We had two different workers who were key people but did not perceive themselves as managers. One of them finally became a supervisor after working successfully in that capacity for several years without the title.

We gave her all the responsibilities and the salary—but not the title. She was so afraid of the onus management titles implied, she repeatedly refused to take the job of supervisor. We gradually gave her more responsibility and more salary until she was functioning in that capacity. Her fourth year on the job she asked to attend supervisors' meetings and she finally accepted the title.

Plan Ahead for Promotions

Many small companies lose potentially good people because they don't plan ahead for promotions. A manager may see great potential in workers and fill vacant positions in haste, promoting people before they're ready. Sometimes this works. Often it doesn't. When it doesn't work, it is important for the manager to handle the situation so the workers don't lose face and the company doesn't lose workers.

It is important for you to admit that you, not the workers, were responsible for the mistake. You gave too much responsibility at this time. You need to assure them you still have confidence in their ability to do the job, but you feel they will ultimately do better after they have had more time to prepare for it. You think it would be a good idea if they returned to their old job for the time being.

Sometimes workers will ask to be taken out of their new jobs. If they do, thank them for their help and point out how much good they have done and how much you appreciate their efforts. Be sure to offer them their old job. Point out that trying the new job was good because it gave them an opportunity to gain additional experience and broaden their background. Let them know workers who are willing to try new things are always valued more. It's important to build their confidence and boost their morale to offset any feeling of inadequacy or failure. Remember, even if they didn't perform to your expectations, they tried.

If the old job is not available, offer a new one that represents the same status and salary or, better yet, more status and salary. If you can offer a job that has more appeal or is more interesting, offer it. Reward the workers in some way to show appreciation for what they tried to do for you, even if it didn't work out. Point out to them and other coworkers how much the company appreciates the efforts of all employee who are willing to try new jobs.

It is vitally important that no stigma be attached to anyone who tries a new job and doesn't succeed. Emphasize the positive aspects of the project. If there is any blame, shoulder it yourself. After all, it was your mistake, not the employee's. Everyone will save face this way. As a manager, you already know the importance of admitting mistakes.

ADMIT MISTAKES

Admit mistakes and you learn faster. Most learning is a gradual process of trial and error. When trainees are acquiring new skills, it's important that their mistakes be acknowledged so they can correct them and learn from them. They need to admit them first. When people admit mistakes you are certain they see them.

A good example is a secretary who worked for our company and was doing an adequate job but had the potential to do much better. Everyone liked her. She wanted so desperately to succeed and to please that she could never admit a mistake. Instead of learning from her mistakes, she spent time defending herself and denying any mistakes had been made. Her excuses were usually that she had been told something else, or she didn't hear, or she didn't know anything about it, or it never happened. Consequently, it was difficult to teach her. After making certain she was given instructions and examining her behavior, we realized she was insecure. She was so eager for others to respect her and admire her work that she was afraid to admit when she did something wrong. She was afraid she would lose the respect and admiration of her coworkers.

We solved the problem by getting her to agree to the following experiment. It may work for you when you encounter this problem. Whenever she made a mistake and admitted it, we praised her and gave her a small bonus. We were careful to explain to her why it was important to admit mistakes as part of the learning process. If she didn't admit a mistake, we gave her a written warning instead. The experiment worked almost immediately. She began admitting mistakes and learning from them. Consequently, she made fewer mistakes. As she developed and began to feel more comfortable with us and the company, she felt more secure. She knew we all made mistakes and we all freely admitted them. Within a short period, she was not only admitting her mistakes she began admitting mistakes that weren't hers. If an error in the office was discovered before anyone could admit the mistake, she would say, "I may have done it without thinking." We were so impressed with her progress she was promoted to executive secretary.

If you freely admit your own mistakes while you're training supervisors, they will follow your example and quickly develop the habit themselves. You'll find it is easier to get them to admit their own mistakes than to report the mistakes of others. Our society teaches us to feel guilty about reporting other people's mistakes. We even have names for people who do it: "tattletale" and "squealer."

To offset this basic reticence in people, we developed a program in our company that proved effective. It was based on our basic belief system and is discussed in detail in the next chapter. I'll mention several techniques you might employ to help people see the importance of reporting mistakes.

How to Deal with Mistakes

The first relates to your attitude toward mistakes, how you deal with them. If you act as if a mistake is a major fault with an employee, that it was deliberate or gross carelessness, you will have a problem getting anyone to admit or report mistakes. If you lose your temper, correct them in public, or in any way make them feel inferior and insecure, you will have problems with mistakes.

Have an attitude that we all make mistakes. It's a natural part of life. It's also a natural part of work. Mistakes are mishaps, accidents; not deliberate offenses. Your first job as a manager is to develop the habit of admitting your own mistakes and reporting others' mistakes. Your second job as a developer of managers is to help others develop that same habit. First, teach them to change their attitude. They must begin to view mistakes from a different perspective, to see them as mishaps or accidents—not as deliberate offenses.

You will encounter careless workers who will make more mistakes than others. If you have done your job of training supervisors to follow through with company policies regarding quality, you'll find the careless workers will soon improve, or they will go to another company where the standards are lower. If you handle the situation correctly, your people won't view mistakes as unimportant. They will view them realistically. They are important, but they are not a reason to denigrate anyone who makes them.

Maintaining Quality

The second aspect relates to quality. Convince your trainees that it's important to report mistakes to maintain and improve quality. You need to know when things go wrong so you can correct them. Show them instances when prompt action reporting a mistake resulted in maintaining or improving quality. Also, award bonuses for reporting mistakes as we did.

Set a Good Example

The third technique you can use when you train managers is to set a good example yourself. Whenever you have to discuss a mistake or a weakness of one of your trainees, use that as an opportunity to tell about one of your own. Don't make them think it doesn't matter, but let them see that making a mistake is a natural part of the process of gaining experience.

MEET FREQUENTLY

Meet frequently with your supervisors. No matter how small your company is, you need to meet in a quiet place to communicate. Weekly staff meetings should do several things: give information about current and new projects; introduce new ideas and projects; and present problems for solutions.

How you approach the discussion of problems and solutions in your meetings can make a difference as to the final outcome and especially to the attitude of your supervisors. Terminology can play a part. Rather than talk about "problems," you may want to call them "situations." We did. Doing so creates a safeguard so meetings don't become gripe sessions. The object is to present matters so that they become a learning device not an excuse to complain.

Weekly Meetings

Our company held weekly supervisors' meetings. Each meeting consisted of two segments. The first part of the meeting was devoted to learning something new about supervision from formal management books. This segment took about fifteen minutes and was presented by one of the supervisors. That supervisor selected the topic and prepared the lesson, then presented it in a format all of us could understand. We all had to participate, and we all learned from it.

The second part of the meeting was devoted to solving daily problems. We called them "situations." Each supervisor would describe at least one problem or situation encountered that week. When we began this program, the supervisors needed my guidance and were seeking my answers. We found by discussing issues together that we were able to arrive at common sense solutions together, by describing situations and sharing them.

Later, supervisors described situations and I would ask them what their common sense told them to do. The supervisors soon arrived at their own common sense solutions without help. As we all became better managers, we described situations and asked trainees how they would handle them—before giving our answers.

We discussed the results and ramifications of our decisions and how we implemented those decisions. Then we wrote them down so we would have a permanent record of each situation, solution, and common sense approach that was used. (See Figure 15.)

You have seen evidence of our situation solution reports throughout this book. We found our supervisory and management skills improved with this technique. Most often the supervisors collectively solved their own problems.

When I introduced this program I used an analogy. I told the supervisors it would be like medical doctors who discuss unusual cases with other doctors. They learn from one another because each of them has knowledge and experience that is different. Collectively, they have a better chance of solving their problems. We found this was true in management too.

Semi-Annual Meetings

In addition to weekly meetings, you need to have dinner meetings once or twice a year if you can. We had quarterly dinner meetings. The company paid for the dinner and for the time the supervisors spent at the dinner meeting. This may sound costly, but it paid dividends for us. All of us felt privileged to have a chance to get together in a different setting and be treated to a special night out. You may want to adopt the method we used.

It's best if you jointly select a restaurant and schedule dinner at a time and place where you have access to a meeting room where you can dress up if you want to. We found everyone wanted an excuse to dress up.

After the dinner, have one or two of the supervisors present a program you have jointly selected for the meeting. This gives the supervisors experience speaking and conducting a meeting in a more formal setting. If two can work on it together, it doesn't seem as intimidating. The meeting should include a brief presentation of the management subject they have selected. Follow this with a brief discussion and a quick quiz on the material. The formal meeting room will keep the meeting on track. The total time for the dinner and meeting should not take more than three hours. Set a time limit. Then if some of the managers want to stay afterward they will know they are on their own.

Figure 15
SITUATION REPORTS

Situation: Before we developed our calendar for the department listing our jobs for the month, the other supervisor and I did things as we thought of them, like ordering supplies. One time I forgot to order temperature cones for the kiln and she didn't order them either, and we ran out.
Solution: We got a calendar and listed our jobs for the month. Every day we check it to make sure we do everything that is listed.

> Common Sense Approach: When there are two of you doing the same job, don't assume the other person is doing what you forgot. Communicate. Jointly make a list for each of you to follow.

Situation: As a supervisor I have five people in my department. I have a problem concerning production flow in our area. I have tried several things to resolve it. None of them has helped. It's just not running as smoothly as it should.
Solution: I called a meeting of the department and explained the situation to them. I asked them for their ideas and suggestions. I was surprised at the ideas they came up with that I hadn't thought of. I found part of our problem is a result of the inefficiency of another department and I wasn't aware of it.

> Common Sense Approach: Discuss departmental problems with your people and invite them to help you solve them. It will improve your department and their individual performance.

Seminars and Other Training

Send supervisor trainees and managers to seminars. Our company sent every supervisor trainee to one seminar sometime during the first six months of their training. These seminars were usually presented by an outside management group sponsored by a university or an association.

Use management training books, and develop some of your own. This is a good way to teach new managers to plan, to think, and to write. Our initial training period was three to six months. Yours may need to be longer. We felt it was a year or more before a supervisor was a seasoned manager.

STRUCTURE

Structure your management training program to ensure success. It is easier for trainees to acquire new duties if you relinquish them gradually. One of the most difficult tasks for managers who train other managers is to give up duties gradually so others can learn to assume responsibilities and take control. The most common excuse is "I can do it faster" or "I can do it easier" or "I can do it better." Of course you can.

Your basic task is to instill confidence in your trainee. You want the trainee to have the opportunity to make decisions and to make mistakes while you are there to guide and counsel. If you continue doing all the tasks or do them sporadically and then suddenly walk away, you are inconsistent and you damage the trainee by creating an unpredictable environment.

Segment Tasks and Delegate

To prevent this, segment tasks and delegate portions of them to the trainee. You might allocate a portion of your daily duties to the trainee while you assume the others. Then trade tasks. This is a good check on the trainee's progress and gives you another point of view when you return to the other tasks. Outline those areas of control you will be relinquishing. List the tasks and point them out as you perform them to acquaint the trainee with each one. Later, assign portions of them. As the trainee performs them successfully, add others. As soon as the trainee is performing all the tasks, have the trainee make the list and keep it. Then let go of the duties. (See Figure 16.) Use daily training reports from the trainee and from yourself. After the trainee is working successfully, space the reports to weekly, then monthly. Praise whenever possible and limit your criticism to constructive comments. This builds confidence as the trainee assumes more responsibilities.

At first, it's more trouble to train and teach than it is for you to continue doing the duties yourself. If you spend extra time now, you will save time later because all you will need to do is follow through on what your trainees do. You can move on to other tasks yourself. Remind the trainees that you cannot promote them until they have developed a person as a replacement. This puts the responsibility on them to develop assistants in their department the way you are developing them as supervisors. Rather than fearing a coworker in their department as a competitor, they will be viewing the person as a possible replacement for themselves so they can be considered for a bigger job in the future.

Figure 16
PLANT MANAGER CHECKLIST

1. Are production goals being met by department?
2. Do we have enough people in each department to meet goals?
3. If we are behind, what steps are being taken to catch up?
4. Are we meeting our shipment goals and if not, why (by project)?
5. Are we meeting our dollar goals?
6. Is each department keeping its costs in line?
7. Are we having quality problems?
8. Are we having people problems?
9. Quality problems:

Planning Ahead

You also need to teach others how to plan ahead. Managers need to plan ahead if they want to avoid problems. When managers don't plan ahead, workers aren't properly trained for emergencies, supplies aren't delivered on time, and production quotas aren't met. Planning ahead pays off when dealing with people, when dealing with other companies, and when introducing new machines, new products, or new policies.

Teach trainees to plan ahead when you introduce new machines. They learn to plan by watching you. They will only be as good as you teach them to be. If you don't have a plan for introducing new machines you may want to develop one.

If you want machines to be used and maintained properly, it is necessary to give careful training. There are several factors to consider: the operation or use of the machine, daily care, scheduling for its use, and maintenance. It does no good to train on one or two aspects and then leave the others to chance. One of these left to chance can result in trouble with the machine.

The first thing to teach trainees is how to teach others to use the machine. Tell them why and how it is important, explain its use, demonstrate it, then train them to use it. Part of that training has to include proper care, checking, and maintenance.

Scheduling

Scheduling is also important when you are training others to introduce machines. When we introduced computers in our company, we found we could operate effectively with fewer computers by doing a better job of scheduling. We observed the times when the computers were not being used and the times when people were waiting to use them.

We checked with each person to find out when they needed the computer the most and the least. We made a schedule that accommodated each person and assigned a specific time for use on certain computers. Teach your trainees to plan and implement this type of program, emphasizing the importance of scheduling.

Introducing New Policies

The next time you have to institute an unpleasant policy, share in the planning with your supervisors and trainees. If your company is like most, you are faced with the problem of instituting a no-smoking policy, a new OSHA standard, or some other policy that has you concerned. You can make this an opportunity to develop people.

There are two ways to introduce a new project or solve a problem. A manager can call a general meeting and explain what has to be done and assign tasks and ask for volunteers. Another common sense approach is to call a meeting of your managers and ask them to help you plan it. Let them know you need their ideas.

There are several advantages to the latter method. By asking for their help you discover how they honestly feel about it. You get ideas from each other about how to solve the problem. You get their cooperation because they are making the decision with you. They have a vested interest in making it work. They respect you more for sharing your problem with them than they would if you had just told them what to do. Later, you can give them credit for helping solve the problem and introducing the new project.

Show your trainees how winning cooperation from all employees must begin with key people. You can handle doubts better in a small group. If you have an unpleasant message to deliver, don't do it in a general meeting until you have announced it to key people to get their response. Otherwise, one negative response can affect others before you have a chance to resolve their doubts. If you teach them to handle it in this way they needn't fear instituting new policies.

In Your Absence

A good opportunity for teaching trainees to plan ahead and work completely on their own is when you are gone for a short time. This will test you too, because no matter how smoothly your business runs when you are there every day, you think it can't run as smoothly when you're gone. You will be surprised to learn that it can—if you plan wisely and teach others how to plan.

Here are several steps to take to ensure everything runs smoothly when you're gone. First, examine the expertise of your people. The more experienced the worker, the less detailed the instructions and training have to be. For example, a new worker or new manager needs more detailed instructions and training sessions than an experienced person. A more experienced manager can be given a list of duties with a short discussion about each.

Whether it's an experienced manager with a list or a new trainee with detailed instructions, people need to be told why tasks are important and how the tasks relate to the overall picture. People are more apt to carry out instructions accurately if they know why and how items relate to a larger task. When you are giving instructions, leave time for questions. You can never be sure someone is absorbing everything if you don't get any questions from them. Ask open-ended questions the way you do when you interview to hire applicants.

A second step is to have a general meeting with the key people and go over the various lists, so each person understands how his or her duties fit into the overall management of the business while you're gone. Provide ample opportunity for your key people to ask questions. Let them second guess your answers. You want them to discover answers for themselves. Discuss what problems they think might surface while you're gone.

Finally, make certain everyone knows they can call you for emergencies. Leave your phone number with the key people and make sure they know help is only a phone call away. You will feel better and so will they.

You can use your absence to motivate your key people. Offer bonuses, pay raises, and promotions based on job performance during your absence. Point out that this is a good test of their abilities to function while you're gone. Leaving someone in charge while you are gone is another opportunity for your trainees to gain more skills and more confidence.

Sharing in Decision-Making

You also want your trainees to learn to make tough decisions. Have you ever wished your subordinates had to make decisions about their pay, their job performance, or their behavior problems? Why not let them share in making decisions? We did and we had a good experience with that approach.

Have financial meetings with your supervisors and key people; let them know what money is available for bonuses and pay raises. They will know firsthand how the company is doing and when the company is having cash flow problems, so they can share in some of the decision making regarding salaries.

We found our key people were qualified to help arrive at a pay scale for themselves. Go over your company's financial situation, their personnel records, and what they plan for their future with the company. After examining their plans with them in the context of the company's, say, "With all this as background and what you have done so far this year, what do you think you should be making right now?" We found the person will suggest a lesser amount than we would have.

You can also use this approach if you have encountered any behavior problems with workers. If you haven't been able to resolve them, call them in and make them share in the decision about what to do. Ask, "What would you do if you were me?" They will usually say, "I guess I would fire me." You can answer with, "But I don't want to fire you because I still believe in you. What can I do to make you believe in yourself and to perform at the level I know you're capable of?" The worker will suggest a harsher solution than you would have.

LET GO

Let go of your duties as you develop people. A common mistake managers make is holding onto a job or certain duties too long. The ones managers are most apt to cling to are those they enjoy the most or, paradoxically, those they like the least but fear no one else can do as well. They are so uncomfortable with the task they can't perceive anyone else doing it with ease, so they refuse to let it go.

You can be good at delegating duties in every respect, but if you don't let go at the proper time you stunt the growth of your trainees. I was guilty of this the last two years I worked at our company. I couldn't bring myself to let go of my personnel duties, even though I felt the time I spent on those duties was not as productive as the time I spent writing. There were others in the office who could have performed those duties, but I insisted on keeping them to myself. I justified my actions by saying the hiring process was critical to the business.

I finally realized I was guilty of the weakness I had seen in other managers. I decided to let go of just one segment of the job in personnel—placing ads. After I let go of that duty and discovered the company didn't collapse, I let go of other duties until I had no personnel duties. You can do it, too.

The best test to see if you are holding onto a task too long is to look for phrases such as, "I'm fearful no one else can do it as well as I can" or "The company might suffer if I don't do it." The exaggerated importance in your life for single tasks are clues for you to let go. If you have used phrases like these to justify any of the tasks you have not relinquished, take a hint—let go. Your need to hang on can become a "hang-up."

8.

How to Project the Right Image

If your company is to succeed, you need to have a good image of yourself first so that you project a good image to your employees. How they feel about you determines how well they work for you and your company. What they say about your company will affect your image in your community. How your company deals with others determines the image you project to your industry, your vendors, and your customers.

Projecting the right image is important for your company's success. You need to be concerned with: (1) yourself, (2) your employees, (3) your community, (4) your industry, (5) your vendors, and (6) your customers.

YOURSELF

How you feel about *yourself* and what you are doing is the biggest determining factor in how others will feel about you. Your personal image will be projected by everything you do. If your self-image is poor, your behavior will quickly unmask your weaknesses. If your self-image is good, your behavior will just as quickly reveal your strengths.

Your attitude and behavior set the standard for everyone else who works for you. You set the example with the language you use, the way you dress, and your general demeanor. If you want your people to take their work seriously, you need to behave in a sincere and earnest manner—not solemn or somber but genuine and straightforward. You cannot act in a frivolous or cavalier manner and expect your employees to take what you say seriously.

You need to be predictable. If you act cheerful and cooperative one day and discontented and irritable the next, you make others around you uncomfortable and insecure. If you want your employees to leave their troubles at home, you need to set an example by keeping your personal problems out of the office.

Working with a Relative or Friend

If you have a business partner and that partner is a close friend or relative, you need to have an agreement at the beginning of your business relationship that your personal lives will remain personal. The major ingredient of our success as a husband and wife team is our ability to separate our business and personal lives. I cannot give you advice on how to do that, but I can give you characteristics and traits we have that may be the secret of our success. They would apply whether your partner is a close friend, a relative, or a spouse.

We have a mutual trust and respect for each other as individuals. If you do not trust or respect someone, you cannot work with that person. We recognize that each of us has talents that are unique. If you do not believe that your business partner is intelligent and can carry his or her end of the business, your partnership will not endure. We each do our own jobs the best we can and leave the other person's job alone. If you cannot stay in your own area of expertise but instead meddle in your partner's, you are doomed as business associates. And finally, we do not confuse personal feelings with business opinions. If you use your personal life to "get even" or your business life to "show off," your relationship won't last.

Setting the Example

Whether your company represents a partnership or not, you need to be aware of the example you set. Since we emphasized good attendance and good attitude we tried to exhibit those traits. We never took days off in the work week. We rarely came to the office late. If we did, we stayed late to make up our time. We never expected anything of our employees that we didn't require of ourselves. We went a step further and worked longer hours than we required of anyone else.

When we went on business trips we worked twelve- and fourteen-hour days. Our employees knew it because the secretaries and office staff had our itinerary. We stayed at the best hotels we could afford, but we never spent money foolishly. We took our clients to dinner at the finest restaurants, but we avoided lavish entertaining at nightclubs and bars.

When we returned from a business trip, we came directly to the office from the airport. We never went home first. It was still a work day for us, and we knew we had mail waiting at the office. Most important, we never complained. We were eager to get to work each day and we acted that way. We enjoyed our work and what we were doing. We were happy, and we wanted happy people around us. We had an image we wanted to project and never lost sight of it.

You need to know what you want to project. Is your small business a service company? Who are you working with? Do you need to wear business suits to work? Or can you wear casual clothes? Do you need to have an impressive office or plant to impress your clients? You can be conservative without being stuffy. But know what you want to be.

We had to wear business suits and maintain a more traditional environment in our company because of the clients with whom we worked. Even though we had a more conventional atmosphere, everyone who visited our company commented on how happy and enthusiastic everyone was. Our managers were constantly striving to maintain the image they knew was important for our company. (See Figure 17.)

YOUR EMPLOYEES

How *your employees* feel about you and respond to your company will determine how well they work for you. They can go through the motions and work at jobs, but if you really want a quality product or service, your employees need to perceive their work as careers—not as "just jobs." The actual work you do is not as important as the way you *perceive* the work you do. I know some university professors with doctorates who have "jobs" and some waitresses with a high school education who have "careers."

How you approach your work is determined by the image you have of yourself and your employer. Your job is to project as good an image as you can, so that your employees will feel good about you, about themselves, and about the jobs they are doing as employees of your company.

Figure 17
SITUATION WITH NEW SECRETARY

On Tuesday I called the new secretary into my office about the dress that she had worn to work that day. It was a short dress that was considerably above the knee and several people had commented about it. I told her that we had explained to her what was proper office attire, and the dress that she had on did not fit into that category. It looked like a dress that a very, very young person would wear and it was not a businesslike dress. I explained that Mr. Tway gets teased a lot because of the fact that we have young girls working here.

I told her that the way she dresses has a lot to do with that and that we all try very, very hard to look mature and act mature and businesslike and that the dress she wore made her look like a "teeny-bopper." She apologized and said that she was embarrassed about it and said that it would not happen again.

I have heard it said repeatedly that the attitudes and behavior of workers are a direct reflection of their managers. One boss I remember said if you have problems with your people and wonder what caused them, look in the mirror. I agree with him. You can't expect workers to behave differently from you. You can't expect them to have an attitude different from yours.

Remember to be fair with your employees and they will trust your judgment. They may not always agree with your decisions, but they will understand your need to make them and will work with you. If workers know you are doing your best, they will do their best and you will be successful.

Pay Fairly

One of your first obligations is to make sure you are paying a fair wage. If you don't know what you should be paying, do some checking in industry publications and with your local employment agencies. We had our CPA check for us so that we knew what was the going rate in our area. The region where you live and the general economy in that region determine the pay scale. We found in our area wages were lower than the national average.

Your goal should be to pay on the upper end of what the going rate is. We always paid the union rate for companies of comparable size in our industry. Once you have established the proper amount to pay your people, it's important they know you went to the trouble to check and make sure they were being paid a fair wage. That way, they know you are not arbitrarily setting the wage scale.

The safest way to be sure you are paying your workers correctly is to become acquainted with your local wage and hour office. I wish we had done this when we first started our business. Instead, we listened to business advisors who told us to keep a low profile. They also gave us incorrect information about wage and hour laws—or we misunderstood what they said. This would not have happened if we had gone directly to the agency. The agency gives accurate information, and it's free. We were lucky our mistake wasn't costly—only a few hundred dollars. Many companies aren't so lucky.

Keeping on the Right Side of Wage and Hour Laws

Each year hundreds of companies like yours are investigated for violating wage and hour laws. Investigations are costly in man hours, back wages, and, in some cases, penalty charges. Many companies are guilty of willful violations. But many of them are not. They are simply the victims, as we were, of misinformation. Their accountant or attorney may have been negligent in checking personnel practices or misinformed about wage and hour laws. To be safe, every employer should know some basic facts about wage and hour laws. Here are some examples of what can happen when you don't. You need to know so you won't make the same mistakes these small business owners made.

One, a manufacturer, developed the habit of letting some employees come in early and others stay late. It was their idea, not his. He told them he didn't need them to work overtime, but if they wanted to do it on their own they could. But if they did, he said they should only report eight hours on their time cards.

When an employee was fired and reported what the company was doing to the wage and hour office, a compliance officer visited the company, examined the records for the past two years (required by law), and interviewed current and former employees of two years' tenure (also required by law). A majority of the employees testified against the employer, and he was held accountable for violating wage and hour recordkeeping laws and had to pay overtime wages to several employees covering a two-year period. Due to his ignorance of the law, the wage and hour office knew it was not deliberate, so he didn't have to pay an additional penalty fine, but it cost his company over a hundred thousand dollars.

After a company is investigated, it is closely watched for the next two years. If there is any violation similar to the previous one, the company is fined because there is clear evidence that the company acted willfully.

What can you learn from this? Keep accurate records of hours your employees work and pay overtime wages if they work more than an eight-hour day. The minimum standard for overtime wages is one and one-half times the hourly wage.

What about your salaried employees? You must keep time cards on them too, unless they are exempt from overtime wages because of the duties they perform. Wage and hour definitions make it clear that titles are not important. It is the duties that a person performs—or does not perform—that determine whether or not the employee is exempt from overtime wages.

Here is a case that illustrates just that. A financial advisor hired two women as office managers and paid them salaries without overtime pay. One of them quit and reported him. His company was investigated and fined. No one was more surprised than the owner, who thought because he "paid them a good salary" and they were "office managers," they were exempt from overtime wages. They were not.

The duties they performed are similar to those of many secretaries, administrative assistants, purchasing agents, and supervisors. Unless 80% of their time is spent on administrative duties if they work for a retail company, or 62% if they work for a non-retail company, they are considered non-exempt professionals and must be paid overtime for work over forty hours in a five-day work week.

What about other professionals such as artists and writers? If an employee is engaged in original, creative work, he or she is exempt from overtime wages. However, there is a fine definition about what is considered "original." If an artist renders a piece of artwork as the result of using a photograph or line drawing to copy or refer to, that is *not* considered an original piece of art. The employer must pay the artist overtime wages for hours worked beyond forty hours in a five-day work week. That's the mistake we made. We inferred from our advisors that artists were exempt. In many cases, they are not. To be safe, check it out.

The most embarrassing cases are ones that involve small companies that employ relatives who may not be competent. One typical case is a manufacturer who employed a relative as an accountant and relied on him for wage and hour advice. The accountant told the owner it was not necessary to pay overtime wages to purchasing agents because they were salaried. The purchasing agents routinely worked more than eight hours a day. One agent became dissatisfied and reported the company. They were investigated and had to pay back wages. Even though the owner promised to get a new accountant and said the fault wasn't his, he was still held accountable. His accountant had assured him everything was OK when in fact it wasn't. His company was breaking a wage and hour law regarding overtime wages of non-exempt workers.

So what to do? Visit your nearest wage and hour office. Ask for brochures or pamphlets covering laws for various types of jobs you have in your company. If you have questions, ask. The wage and hour people are there to help you. They will even give seminars to educate your staff. Their advice can save you money and embarrassment, and best of all, their advice is free.

EEOC, OSHA, and Worker's Compensation Compliance

You also need to get advice from the EEOC, OSHA, and Worker's Compensation offices. You need to know what is required of you as an employer in your industry, including what posters to display. These requirements change and you must keep informed.

You may have worked in your industry for many years before

starting your small business. But unless you worked closely with the industrial relations director, you can't be sure your information is accurate. My husband had worked for years in our industry in sales and marketing but had no knowledge of OSHA standards. My work with the industrial relations director during my doctoral research alerted me to the pitfalls that await any business that doesn't comply with all government standards regulating industries. That's why we were careful to check with them frequently. If you have a small business, it's easy to take a positive and aggressive approach toward providing a safe place to work. You have fewer people to worry about maintaining your high standards.

The OSHA office exists to help employers provide the safest, cleanest workplace they can for their employees. Keep the rules and you will have no problems. But first, find out what the rules are and how they apply to your company. Do this with the other government agencies such as Worker's Compensation and EEOC. We had no problems with Worker's Compensation except that our insurance advisors inadvertently told us to use claim forms for accident reports. We discovered it several years after we started our business. We had very few accidents and the majority of them were cut fingers that required only minor medical attention. If you have a small business, you probably don't have a nurse or doctor on call. That's why you need to take the injured person to the emergency room of your local hospital to have the employee checked. We were careful to have any injury looked at in the emergency room of our local hospital. We only had three or four claims in the fourteen years we operated our business. We were not so lucky with the EEOC. I will relate our experience to show that you can do everything right and still have an unfair claim against you.

I fired a young woman for high absenteeism. She had been missing work and had been given two written warnings and repeated verbal warnings. Finally, when she missed work again and the next day admitted that she had attended a hair-dressing class instead of coming to work, I terminated her. She attempted to get unemployment benefits and was denied. She then went to the regional EEOC office and claimed I had fired her for sex discrimination because she was pregnant. I didn't know she was pregnant and had written the reason for discharge as high absenteeism and admission that she had missed work to go to a hair dresser's class. I explained this to the EEOC officer by phone and was told we still had to attend a hearing.

We hired an attorney for consultation only and defended ourselves in the hearing. We won the case, but it was expensive and exasperating to have to defend our position when we were innocent. We showed employee files to prove that we had several young women who worked during their pregnancies and returned after their babies were born. We also showed that the majority of our labor force included supervisors and top managers who were female.

You must realize when you own a small business that you can be charged with anything. Your job is to make sure that your company is organized, that you are specific about what you say and do, and that you document your actions. Only then can you adequately defend yourself against unfair claims.

Here is another example. Another woman with a high absentee rate knew she was on probation and went to OSHA claiming she got sick because of fumes from our kilns. When the OSHA investigator saw how meticulous our housekeeping was, he was apologetic for bothering us and invited me to give talks for OSHA if I ever had the time.

A final example is the false claim to the steelworker's union by two workers who said we fired them because they were trying to organize a union. This was not true, as the representative of the National Labor Relations Board soon discovered. It was then we received the compliment from the NLRB that I wrote about in the beginning of the book.

If charges are leveled against you, defend your actions and back up your statements with employee records showing you are a fair employer who keeps all the government rules. It is best if you can also show you go the extra mile for your employees. Then you know you are projecting the right image for your company.

YOUR COMMUNITY

Your image in the *community* is important because you will probably draw your employees from the community in which your business is located. Joining local business and industrial organizations may help you if you are selling your product locally. Otherwise, you may feel you don't have the time, but remember this may be a good way for you to give talks about your product. If the newspaper covers the events, you will get some free publicity.

Your image in the community is more likely to come from employees who work for you. How they feel about you and what they say about you and how many unemployment claims you have against you will do more to give you an image than belonging to some local organizations. For this reason, it's a good idea to keep in touch with the local unemployment office.

There is a misconception among some employers that unnecessary communication with government offices gives your company a high profile and puts you at risk of being treated harshly. We found just the opposite to be true.

Working with the Unemployment Office

The unemployment office exists to help employees and employers have a better relationship. Therefore, it's just common sense to get better acquainted. The best way to do this is to communicate with your unemployment office. It will enhance your company's image now and prove profitable later. Here are some of the things our company did. You may want to do them, too.

Invite one or more unemployment claims examiners to your facility. Give them a tour. Let them see you are a fair employer trying to do the right thing—and that you have nothing to hide. Acquaint them with your policies by letting them see your personnel handbook. Let them know you welcome helpful suggestions to improve your operation.

If they get to know you now, before there is a claim against you, they are in a better position to render a fair decision. They will have a more accurate picture of your company to offset any false negative impression an unfair employee might give. Bad employees you discharge or who quit often misrepresent the facts.

The unemployment office is also more likely to give you valuable information to help document employee problems. Their job is to educate you as well as your employees. If they know you are interested in using them as an employment service, they will screen future employees for you as I discussed earlier.

Ask them if they prefer you work with the same examiner each time you call. Some unemployment offices prefer this method. It is easier for them to remember who you are if one person, rather than several different examiners, is responsible for handling cases from your company.

Contact your examiner immediately after an employee quits or is discharged. Explain what occurred and let them know you have the necessary documentation to support your claim. Your prompt action will help them make a fair decision because it will give them your side of the story before the employee talks with them, since some employees distort the facts. It will also show them you are vitally interested in personnel problems.

Attend all unemployment hearings involving your company. This builds credibility. They will know you care; that you stand behind your policies. Examiners get discouraged when employers don't show up for hearings to support their favorable decisions. If they decide in your favor and the employee appeals, you are obligated to attend the hearing and support the examiner's decision. When you don't, you are implying that either the employee was right and the examiner was wrong, or that it doesn't matter to you. If it doesn't matter to you, why should it matter to the examiner? Next time, it might be easier and less embarrassing for the examiner to decide in favor of the employee—even if he or she may not deserve it—than to spend time making a tough decision that isn't supported by the company.

Remember, if an employer discharges an employee for any reason, the burden of proof is on the employer. If the employer fails to provide the necessary proof for the discharge in writing, then the claimant will be made eligible for unemployment benefits.

If the employer fails to attend a hearing, the claimant will be made eligible despite the original examiner's decision in the company's favor. This is why it is vitally important that you show up for unemployment hearings, especially if the examiner has ruled in your favor and the employee is appealing it.

Appeal every decision you believe is unjust. This builds credibility with the unemployment office and with your employees. Word will get around that you don't carelessly let employees draw unemployment benefits unjustly without a hearing. Unemployment examiners will respect your attitude and give careful attention to your cases—and unfair employees will be less likely to take advantage of you in the future. They will know it doesn't pay off.

Educate your employees about unemployment benefits. Most workers erroneously believe all unemployment benefits are paid for by employees, and they deserve them if they lose their jobs for any reason. Explain to your employees that unemployment benefits are paid for by the company and by tax dollars. Those benefits are available only for legitimate reasons, such as layoffs, shutdowns, or unfair discharges. Let employees know they can get details from the unemployment office and that you have a good relationship with that office.

When we first started our company, we made the mistake of listening to business advisors who told us to "keep a low profile" with the state agencies. We inferred from this that we were to keep our distance and only contact them when there was trouble. I soon learned, as I got to know them better after the first year or two, that instead of keeping our distance we should have gotten better acquainted with our state agencies at the beginning.

Over the next twelve years our relationship with the local unemployment office developed into a good one. They knew, and our employees knew, that we were fair but firm in our personnel policies—we stood behind them. We had very few claims against our company, and when we did, we almost always won. On rare occasions when we lost, we appealed and won. No one can win 100% of the time, but you can cut your losses if you try and if the agency knows you have the right attitude.

We discovered that the more the unemployment office knew about us, our company, and the way we ran it, the more successful we were in our relationship with them and with our employees. They knew the truth about us and supported us when we had problems or questions.

I believe you will have the same experience if you get acquainted with your unemployment office. It will simplify your personnel problems now and save your company money later. It will certainly enhance your image in the community.

YOUR INDUSTRY

Your image with the *industry* is important because it can directly and indirectly affect your business. Others in the industry may recommend you for things they can't do or are too busy to do. Over the years, we got several accounts this way. Your reputation with the industry also has an indirect effect on your business. When customers hear others in the industry talk about you, it helps cement their relationship with you—if what is said about you is good.

Attend Trade Shows

Attend trade shows when you can. You'll learn more about the competition and what they're doing. It will also let them know you exist. Their customers will have an opportunity to see your work and compare it with your competitors'. Attending trade shows need not cost you a great deal of money. While some companies spend hundreds of thousands of dollars for display booths, you can make one yourself, or have it made, for much less. We saw a number of trade booths we liked when we visited trade shows before we started exhibiting. When we found booths we liked, we took pictures and made notes so we could borrow ideas from them.

Our first trade booth was composed of 4' x 8' wooden panels covered with a short napped carpet and hinged so the panels folded to become free standing. We used carpet covered barrels to match. The barrels provided a place to display our product line at the show and a place to store the product when we were ready to ship. We had an elegant brass logo made and hung it in the center of the booth.

We always rented lights, floor carpet, and a telephone at the show and made sure there were colorful flowers in the booth. The total cost to build our booth was about a thousand dollars but looked much more expensive. Later we bought collapsible booths that had the same appearance but were much lighter to ship. Whatever you decide to do, make your booth as attractive as you can.

Join Associations

You also should join industry associations. This can be a good way to learn more about your industry and build a network of contacts. If you are invited to serve on a committee that can help your business, do so. If you are asked to serve as chairman and you can do it without taking too much time from your work, do so. It will help build your image in the industry.

Attend association meetings and give presentations about your company's product or processes. Talk about your business or product at some of the roundtable discussions and attend association seminars to increase your knowledge of the industry. It is another way to get better acquainted with your competitors. As competitors, you can view each other as adversaries, be secretive, and refuse to share ideas. Or you can view each other as colleagues, be open, and communicate with one another. Naturally, the latter approach is the most productive one. It is the one generally taken by the most successful people in any industry or profession. It is the approach we tried to take at our company.

Learn from Competitors

We learned many of our production techniques from the china company that had sponsored my doctoral dissertation and permitted me to publish a number of articles about their operation. I mentioned the lasting effect their union president had on me and the knowledge I received from their industrial relations director. When we began our company, a number of their key people helped us with ideas and suggestions. We considered them colleagues and valued their friendship and advice. When visiting other plants here and abroad we often discussed personnel policies, if only informally. Learning something about how others in the industry hire, manage, and train their employees can be a great asset when setting up or streamlining your own policies.

We never visited another plant that I didn't take a camera and ask to photograph different work areas. How others place machines, store items, or set up work flow can give you ideas about how to arrange your own work area. Only twice did any company refuse to let me photograph inside their plants. Both times pertained to the development of new machinery, which brings me to the subject of proprietary information.

Communicating and sharing ideas doesn't mean telling trade secrets. If you are working on a new project with a client, don't discuss it with anyone unless you know your client approves. There is such a thing as privileged information. But the sharing of basic techniques and general information is necessary for companies, and for your industry as a whole, in order to thrive and grow.

Another thing we borrowed from competitors was our arrangement of space. The Japanese are especially adept at saving space. When they can't expand their facilities outward, they expand them upward. So when we needed more warehouse space, rather than build a new building or renting another one, we bought heavy industrial shelving and doubled-decked our warehouse. By doing this, we doubled our warehouse space, made taking inventory easier, and gave a more orderly appearance to the work area.

I sometimes think we had a fetish about cleanliness because of the Japanese. I mentioned previously how we had our entire facilities cleaned each day. The floors were scrubbed and polished each night and the walls painted frequently. This all came about because we saw how it benefited the Japanese factories and their workers. It may seem costly and time consuming, but it is worth it from the standpoint of your product, your people, and your image. We found employees work better, take more interest in every job they perform, and consequently produce a better product when they work in a clean, orderly environment. They are also more eager to experiment with new techniques.

When we visited factories in England, the Netherlands, Portugal, and Germany, we learned new ways to store paints and supplies. When we returned, we instituted some of their procedures. The way we stored some of our most expensive decal was taught to us by major decal suppliers. Utilizing inexpensive file cabinets for small amounts of decals and for samples was suggested to us by a small decorating plant like ours.

We borrowed several important marketing concepts from our competitors, especially overseas competitors. My husband spent all his business life in marketing and sales. As president of our company, he felt it was necessary to learn from and work with our overseas competitors. In fact, we shared some projects with them. But first we tried to place the projects with other American companies. Usually when we could show a customer that American manufacturers in our industry could give better delivery dates, and a "made in USA back-stamp," they preferred these advantages to a cheaper price.

An important marketing approach we borrowed from the Japanese was to put the customer's demands first. This was contrary to what most American manufacturers in our industry were doing when they refused to try new things for customers.

Another concept we borrowed from our competitors was to keep a vigilant eye on the changing market and be aware of how and where our particular expertise fit; in other words, keeping an eye on our marketing niche.

Competition is good. It gets the marketplace interested in your kind of product and literally blazes a path for you. I remember years ago my husband and I worked for a large conglomerate that deliberately stimulated the marketplace by creating its own competition. At one time they owned nineteen different companies with identical or similar markets. They were all very successful.

Each of us owes a great deal to our competitors for what we can learn from them, whether in talking on the phone, visiting other plants, or meeting at association conferences. We all have opportunities to learn if we keep our minds open and are willing to share ideas.

Industrial societies that bring competitors together as colleagues provide many opportunities for you to learn more about each other and your industry. Take advantage of these opportunities, in general sessions, workshops, and between-meeting visits, to communicate and to learn. You will be better for it, and it will improve your image.

YOUR VENDORS

Vendors who supply you with products you need to operate are important to you. You need to establish good relations with them and project a positive image. You also need to be firm to maintain the quality standards you want from them.

If they know you won't settle for second best, they will be more careful when they ship you something. If they know you need prompt deliveries and that you follow through when they don't ship things on time, they will give you good delivery service. You set the standard for your relationship with vendors.

We wanted to make a good impression on our vendors and made certain they were given a tour of our facilities and saw the awards and commendations we had received from our community and our industry. If they feel you are a quality company, they will take better care of you.

In addition to having vendors visit you, it is a good idea to visit them. See what their facilities look like. Is it a quality organization? Do some checking to be sure you are doing business with a reputable company. We visited our vendors at least once a year. Just getting together and talking about the business established a rapport that fostered good feelings and gave us better service.

YOUR CUSTOMERS

Your image with *customers* will either keep you in business or get you out of it. The major reason you are in business is to satisfy customers. Your job now is to do everything you can to project a good image.

A small business doesn't have a large advertising budget. You have to be creative to get the attention some companies get by sponsoring a golf match or tennis tournament or placing a huge ad in a magazine or newspaper. We didn't have a large advertising budget, so we had to think of other ways to get attention.

We paid a nominal fee to a good public relations director who placed our product in a number of prestigious magazines that we knew our customers read. Whenever there was a trade show, she made sure we were in the magazines that were distributed at those shows and made certain there was some news release about our product.

On two separate occasions, she got us on the covers of major magazines. This is something you can't buy. She kept in close contact with editors to find out if they needed a product like ours for a photographic layout. Because she was alert and we were willing to put something together in a hurry when she needed it, we were able to get in a number of prestigious publications. Our biggest competitors were paying thousands of dollars for full-page spreads in the same magazines in which we were featured on the editorial pages in full color. If she knew an editor needed a product like ours to display another product, she would call us and we would send something appropriate. We got a great deal of free advertising that way.

Another way we got publicity was through articles I wrote for major publications. I always wrote about our product, our company, or some customer who used our product. I took color slides of every department and used the slides in my articles. I also let editors know the slides were available if they ever needed pictures of a clean manufacturing plant.

If you take this route and write articles about your business, you have to be careful and use competitors' products, too. I used the most famous competitors because it was good for us to be in the same article with them. They welcomed the publicity they were getting from the articles too. We borrowed status from their fame, and it didn't cost us anything. Sometimes the publication even paid me for the articles.

Another way we got publicity was through news stories about our product. When I designed the china service for President and Mrs. Carter's fishing lodge, we got a good write-up in *The Washington Post* and *The New York Times*. When I designed the dinner service for the Vice Presidential Mansion and the giftware for Mrs. Quayle, we received publicity from this in general news releases.

When we reproduced the White House Presidential dessert plate series, my husband made sure they were marketed through the Smithsonian and the presidential libraries. He also made sure through his contacts that the plates were given to each former president each year they met for a dinner. He also made a point of selling at least two or three prestigious accounts, each year, so we could talk about them to other customers and get news releases for the general public.

You can also make your product available for presentation awards. We did, and found it an excellent way to become well-known. Whenever an award is given, there is a news release that includes information about the product. It's all free, except for the cost of your product.

If you maintain a clean work environment, you will want to have customers visit your place. Give a guided tour with one of your best people or yourself. Plan ahead and decide what you want to emphasize and write a script that covers all those things. Memorize the script so you give it the same way each time and in a natural manner. You may want a different script for different visitors.

Be sure you have awards and commendations hanging on the walls of your place where the most employees work. We always put all our awards in the plant where most of the workers were. They were proud of those awards because they knew they earned them.

Every worker at the china plant I researched complained that their company had never shown them the finished product. Most of them had worked all their lives in the business and had never seen the fruits of their labor.

We vowed when we started our business that we would put our nicest products in the lunch room where the people who created them could enjoy their beauty. We put products we wanted to sell in the conference room. We put everything else in the plant. Everyone who came to visit was impressed to see how important our employees were to us and to see how proud our employees were of the things they made.

Display and talk about any awards you receive from state or local agencies. We received the Optimum Energy and Load Management awards from Penn Power in our state. We received them for our economical use of energy. It was important for customers to know we were doing everything we could to save them money by saving manufacturing costs. Anything you do to enhance your image with your customers will pay dividends for you.

Every company has a personality of its own. That is its image. It is a combination of all the attributes of the people who make up that organization. The personality of the company reflects the personalities and attitudes of the workers and the managers.

9.

How to Know
You Did It Right

When you start your small business you believe in it and in your abilities to make it successful. No matter what size your business attains before you retire, your personal satisfaction from having done it will make it worth the effort. You will enjoy it more when you know others respond in a positive way. Their response proves your success.

Evidence of your success will come from: (1) satisfaction with yourself, (2) contentment of your people, (3) recognition by your community, (4) prestige in your industry, (5) respect from your vendors, and (6) appreciation from your customers.

SATISFACTION WITH YOURSELF
Satisfaction with yourself is one proof of your success. No matter what the size of your company, if you are happy in your work you are successful. Earlier, I compared the attitudes of professors and waitresses and pointed out that attitude—not the work—made the difference between having a job and having a career. Your attitude—not the size of your company—makes the difference between running a business and enjoying an enterprise.

I have known corporate executives of Fortune 500 companies who were not successful because they did not perceive themselves as successful. No matter how important they became or how large their companies grew, they were never satisfied and never really happy. Conversely, I have known owners of small grocery stores or diners who were successful because they perceived themselves that way. They were exuberant over their jobs and happy to be working at something they created.

What you have done in starting your small business is remarkable. You are providing work for yourself and others while satisfying the needs or desires of people with the service you and your employees provide or the product you make and sell. Knowing this should make you feel lucky every day you come to work and proud of what you have done.

Of course you have bad days. Shipments don't go out on time, deliveries are late, customers misunderstand, and a worker quits. Nothing is ever perfect. You may strive for perfection but be content with excellence. One is always attainable; the other seldom is. Do not denigrate yourself for what you didn't attain today; instead compliment yourself for what you did achieve. It will help you develop the habit of feeling successful.

When things go wrong it is easy to feel dissatisfied. I described several instances when false claims were made against us and how we had to defend ourselves. Those are the times you question what you are doing and why. Is it worth it? It is, when you see positive results from what you are doing. We feel a great deal of satisfaction from what we did—a combination of my husband's marketing expertise and my ability to apply the concepts, methods, and techniques I describe in the book. Let me give you some reasons *we* are satisfied.

After we sold our business and moved to Florida, I asked several key people from our company to write about their work history and anything else they wanted to write about—what they would change or do differently. I had no reason for doing it at the time except as a final sharing of our work together. In fact, when I received their letters I had already completed this book as eight chapters.

I was so impressed with their responses, I asked their permission to include them. It was the impetus for this last chapter. Proof of our success from them prompted me to include proof from the other sources I talked about in Chapter 8. And it gave me the idea for Chapter 9. Once again, sharing with each other helped create something better than I would have created alone. This chapter is my favorite one because it is ours together.

Their responses are proof of what you can expect when you consistently apply the methods and techniques I describe in this book. They will also give you an idea of the lasting effects your mistakes can have on others.

Mistakes I Made

I made many mistakes; some big ones I hope I never make again. That's part of the learning and growing process. I need to relate two of my biggest mistakes before you read the letters because the letters graphically illustrate them.

The first was my inability to develop more young men for our business. This is apparent in the ratio of men to women in the following responses. While we interviewed and hired a number of male applicants, we never had the success with them we had with the females.

I am aware that one reason is our type of work. It attracts more women to the industry, especially our segment. I am also aware that the few men we did develop were exceptional and stayed with us when they could have worked other places for more money and less security.

But I still wonder if the management policies I believe in are more oriented to a female labor force. Even my husband, who now applauds all of them, at first thought a few of my notions were inappropriate in the workplace. He had spent most of his work life in large corporations that advocated totally different ideas: you don't admit mistakes; you guard your territory; and you compete with everyone else on the team if you want to be a winner.

I was promoting notions to admit and report mistakes, share everything, help each other grow, learn each other's jobs, and make people feel more secure. Our women easily adapted to these notions. It seemed natural to them. Our men had more difficulty adapting because the ideas seemed foreign to them. Those young men who did adapt preferred our management and stayed with us. Those who left later said our management policies were the best.

But it still bothers me that these basic concepts are so easy for women to accept and so unnatural for most men to relate to. As an anthropologist and linguist, I can only attribute it to the culture—not the individual. For it was the individual who stepped outside his cultural background to accept our concepts and succeed with our company.

The second mistake was attempting to change the language habits of three employees who worked in sales service. The negative effect of this is evident in the response from one of them.

During our years in business, fewer than two dozen employees had any education beyond high school; three were supervisors, a dozen were office personnel, and the others were artists. None of our top managers had a college degree. I would have preferred it if they had, but I never felt it was necessary in order to be successful. My husband is proof of that. Native intelligence and common sense are just as important as an education. Some of the dullest people I know have PhDs, and some of the sharpest people I know haven't been to college. I'm reminded of a description I heard of a person with several degrees "who speaks six languages and is dumb in all of them."

Our employees spoke only one language and not always correctly. But they were smart. Does language make a difference? The truth is, we evaluate people by the language they use—both body language and verbal language. We tend to classify people by their gestures, grammar, and vocabulary. Knowing all this and teaching it in college, I probably put too much emphasis on it in our business.

As bright and eager as these few sales service employees were, I could never improve their bad grammar. We proofread their letters and made corrections but most of their work with clients was conducted by telephone. Did it matter whether they said, "he don't" and "them ones?" I thought it did because we were trying to project an image of high quality in everything. These young women were talking with important clients, some of whom were at the pinnacle of their profession in industry and government.

All my attempts proved futile. I even agreed to change my speech habits by putting 25 cents in the piggy bank every time I swore if they put 5 cents in the piggy bank every time they used bad grammar. It only succeeded in making them fearful and me frustrated. I admitted my mistake and said I would never attempt such a thing again.

The success they had with our clients despite their bad grammar proves I was wrong. How wrong I was is further illustrated by the letters of commendation we received about our company and our people from the community, the industry, the vendors, and the customers. The image our employees projected for our company leaves no doubt about their success and ours.

But let me tell you more about them and why we feel satisfied with what we did. Their background is typical of many young people who come from America's working class families. They fall into the cracks where education and opportunity for college are concerned. They are not eligible for free tuition by state-supported universities that help children from urban ghettos. Yet their intelligence and abilities make them ideal candidates. They don't have enough money from home to help with their education beyond high school. And they don't receive any motivation or support from any quarter to challenge or encourage them to become the best that they can be.

We were especially proud of one of our first supervisors who had quit school to marry and start a family, then juggled family, full-time job, and night school to get her high school diploma while working for us. Sadly, she was the supervisor I described in Chapter 2 whose husband and mother-in-law made her quit. She had more natural aptitude for numbers than many college students I taught.

Most of these young people, especially the young women, have babies early, either in or out of wedlock, and soon become single parents and the sole support of themselves and their young children. They do not have a college education but are very bright and highly motivated to do their best when someone takes the time and interest to work with them as individuals.

More than one professor who visited our plant said they never saw as much talent in college as we had at our company. They asked where we found such good people. Presidents and managers from our top competitors who visited our plant also asked where we found such talent. One top manager said, "I'll trade ten of my workers for one of yours any day." We had more than one company try to hire our people from us. We were complimented—not threatened—because we knew they wouldn't leave. They were as much a part of the company as we were. Our company was their home and our home for eight hours out of every day, five days a week.

Early on I was so enthused about what we were doing, I published articles about how we trained and how we maintained our quality. Our competitors said, "Aren't you worried to give away trade secrets?" I answered, "No, because most of the readers are from large corporations who won't agree with our ideas."

When people visited us, they commented on several things: how clean everything was, how busy we were, and how happy and motivated everyone seemed. How did we do it? By doing the things I have written about in the preceding pages. We interviewed and hired selectively, trained and developed methodically, and provided a predictable environment that recognized individuals and fostered communication.

Our secret was twofold: we set our own standards and we never compromised them. We tried never to settle for second best. We got fooled sometimes but not often enough to discourage us or make us lower our standards. I'm proud of the employees we developed and I want you to meet some of them in the next section.

CONTENTMENT OF YOUR PEOPLE

Contentment of your employees as manifested in their response is one proof of your success. (See Figure 18.) She is the sales service person we received the most complimentary letters about from our customers.

You met this young woman in Chapter 2 when I discussed the effects of romance at work and her success as a sales service person. We chose her over her boyfriend and knew we made the right decision. You met her again in Chapter 3 as the employee who took applicants on tour and assessed their body language.

Figure 18
SALES SERVICE PERSON

My name is Denise Richman. I started working at Woodmere China when I was in high school. I worked in the evenings, then, after I graduated, I worked full time.

The first thing that I noticed, was how clean the studio was. We didn't allow any smoking or eating in the studio or at any of the supervisors desks, which I thought was very professional looking.

We had working supervisors. You never saw any supervisor just sitting at their desk. They were involved with all of their people. If any problem occurred you knew right when it happened. It wasn't through rumor.

When there was a problem, it was dealt with right away. As Mrs. Tway would say, "You praise in public and reprimand in private" which to this day I believe 100%. All of the supervisors and the managers had an open-door policy. Anytime you wanted to talk to someone with a question or a problem, you were able to.

We had weekly quality control meetings on the cleanliness and the production of the *people*. Everyone knew what they had to meet for production and what was expected of them.

There were two things that we stressed, attitude and attendance. Attitude, we wanted everyone to be happy and like what they're doing. Attendance, because we are small, we do not have the people to fill their position when they're not here. Keeping these two in mind, we find that we have a very good work force.

Figure 18, cont'd.

We did find that we did not have very good success with men. We did find that they are not as hard working and expect more than what they are willing to work for. We found that men have a very hard time taking directions from a female, and some of the females were your best managers. We have also found that they can not take constructive criticism as well as a female. There was also your "male ego" to contend with!

I liked the idea of how I was trained in every position. When I became a supervisor, I knew the whole operation. I knew what to do and what to look for. Being as small as we are, the more people that know the different areas, the more valuable they are to the company.

Mrs. Tway brought out the best in people as far as their capabilities. She said that it was up to each individual on how far they wanted to go in the company. We had yearly evaluations which I thought were great. You would set goals for yourself and you would also work to improve your weaknesses.

I have been through a lot with Mrs. Tway. I feared her at one time! But she was tough with us because she wanted us to be the best we could be. There were only a few of us that were really put through the ringer but each one of us grew the most in the company. We all had highly respected positions and what mattered the most was that our opinion counted for something. We actually were a part of Woodmere China. In the ten years that I have been working, I don't believe that I would change anything that she did. I highly respect Mrs. Tway and I always will.

I feel, from working with Mrs. Tway, that I have very high standards not only just in my working environment but in my personal life.

Denise

You will recognize this next employee from Chapter 5, where I discussed the importance of being flexible and told of her importance to us as night kiln supervisor.

Her remarks also reveal the problem I discussed in the Introduction to the book—the previous bad management of the plant due to a young man we hired to run it when we first started our manufacturing operation and I was working part-time. Her remarks also relate her experiences with me after my husband asked me to join the company full-time to reorganize and run the manufacturing end of the business. This young woman had the endless task of helping me clean up the previous bad manager's messes.

She represents the epitome of a good employee. Instead of waiting for more instructions after she finishes a task, she eagerly asks, "What can I do next?" and she never says, "No." Instead she says, "Let's try." (See Figure 19.)

Figure 19
NIGHT SUPERVISOR

I started with Woodmere on April 4, 1979. For the first few days I worked as a final inspector of plates. We would have to take racks of plates from kilns that had been fired, put them on our table and inspect them. At this time there were plates everywhere in the kiln area. Stacks on floors in all areas and corners, etc.

After about the third day Mrs. Tway came back to me and said she needed a secretary. We went to the front office where she had me start sorting and mailing information cards and brochures. The very next day she came to me and said she had to go into the back to reorganize. I started sorting, counting and organizing decals. They had been scattered everywhere. Mrs. Tway brought me some suitcases of decal to begin working with. Later on we put decals into the front office area in wareboxes on shelves.

Mrs. Tway and I than began sorting inventory of the decorated pieces. I labeled shelves with pattern names and began moving pieces around to where they belonged and took inventory. Mrs. Tway had hired another lady to work with me but she didn't work out. I think the job just overwhelmed her. Once we had the inventory taken we started to process open orders.

Everyday I would go back with the orders, pull decorated ware needed, and lay it in boxes with an order form and then the Shipping Clerk would pack it up and ship it out. After depleting the stock I would then put together a list of items still needed and go over this with Mrs. Tway and then we put it into production by hand writing a production order. This enabled us to keep track of the pieces.

I enjoyed this job because you followed through in each department to make sure things kept moving.

From here I believe my next step was shipping and warehouse. At that time we unloaded full containers of ware by dolly. Now they are skidded, at least most of the time, which makes it easier to stack and unload. I remember when Mr. Tway was working on the bone china orders, we received a shipment and we needed to inspect it for problems. We worked at the warehouse on Route 18. We separated good from bad and reported numbers.

I began filling in for Mr. Tway's secretary when she went on vacation. She trained me to do her duties. I can remember how scary that was and then when she decided to retire I remember Mrs. Tway calling me into the office and asking me if I would step into this position. I accepted knowing that when I wanted, I could go back into the studio.

As Mr. Tway's secretary, I grew in my secretarial skills. Once I got into a routine and more familiar with the dictaphone I felt comfortable in the job. My duties were to answer the telephone, process the mail, take care of items from Mr. Tway's out box, typing & filing. I learned a lot working with Mr. Tway. He bought a Radio Shack computer so we could start putting inventory in the computer. I began making computer codes and entering in descriptions of each item and quantity on hand. As we grew we also advanced to a better system, which today not only holds inventory but

Figure 19, cont'd.

processes orders, accounts receivable, accounts payable and can also do payroll. I believe all companies today run this way.

As our company started growing Mr. & Mrs. Tway decided to add a Sales Department. They hired a woman who tried it. Eventually I began sharing an office with Mr. Tway and listening in on his phone calls and learning how to help customers and follow through on their orders. I liked this job the most out of everything I have done. I enjoyed meeting and talking with our customers, processing their orders and following through with problems and working them out. I probably would still be working in this area except when I decided to get married in 1984 I wanted to concentrate more of my time on a family, and I'm glad I did.

At this point in time I moved back into the Studio. I asked for the packing department because I liked to be up and moving. I eventually moved into the Decorator Supervisor position. In this department my duties were to train and work with the girls to decorate the orders. We were working with some tricky decals but we moved the order through our department.

After I had my baby in 1987 I came back on the nightshift. I ran the kiln dept at night and as we grew more and added decorators at night I moved up into the position of Night Kiln Supervisor and Overseer of the Shift. I believe this is my second best loved job out of everything I have done. I enjoy best working with people and helping them out the best way I can.

(Personal note)—I don't think there is one day that goes by that I don't stop and think about both of you and how wonderful it was to have enjoyed the years we spent together.

Linda Martin

You met the next employee in Chapter 5. She is the employee whose husband's work shift caused baby-sitter problems, and we let her work flexible hours in the decal inventory department. It is evident from her feelings for our company that she appreciated our efforts to help her, although she doesn't single them out. That is what you must accept when you do things for employees. You do them because it is right—not because you expect them to discuss every single gesture you make when they talk about you.

You met her again in Chapter 7. She is the warehouse supervisor who worked at the job for a period of time before accepting the title. My husband and I both agree she is the best warehouse supervisor we have ever encountered anywhere. Her ability to map space and juggle inventory while keeping an accurate count is exceptional. She will make an excellent plant manager. (See Figure 20.)

Figure 20
WAREHOUSE SUPERVISOR

I began my Career, at Woodmere China, in Jan. 1980. I have worked several different jobs, in my past 11 years with the company.

Packing Department. I worked in the packing department, only for a few weeks. In packing I learned how to individually pack commemorative plates and bulk-pack plates. With each commemorative plate packed, I had to make sure the plate number and certificate number matched. I also had to insert a flyer with each plate and certificate. I then had to pack the individual plate boxes into master boxes. Each master box had to be labeled correctly with the amount of plates and with the name of the plates.

Shipping Assistant. I worked as the shipping assistant for about two weeks. The only things she had me do were clean up her messes, and tape boxes, type shipping labels, and help the warehouse supervisor.

Figure 20, cont'd.

Shipping Clerk. When the Shipping Clerk got sick and had to leave the company, I was promoted to the job. Needless to say no one really knew the job. I was always running to Mr Tway and his secretary, asking questions, and learning how to do the job. With their help I succeded in learning the different types of ware, and what pieces of ware go into a set. After about a month I felt I could handle the job. I was responsible for scheduling truck shipments, air shipments, UPS shipments, and Federal Express shipments. I also shipped sample orders, com-memorative orders, crystal orders, and dinnerware orders, and ran tracers on shipments. I checked the incoming shipments, inventoried crystal and dinnerware, and stamped the mail. Along with my Shipping duties, I also learned to assist my Warehouse Supervisor. I learned how to pull ware and do her inventory. When she needed help at the warehouse I went and helped. I did the Shipping job about 8 months when the Warehouse Supervisor left the company.

Warehouse Supervisor. I took over the warehouse supervisor's job, only on a temporary basis, until a replacement could be found. Since I felt I did not know enough about the company, I was uncomfortable with supervising. Mrs Tway was very understanding with how I felt. She did everything possible to find a replacement for the position, but everyone I trained didn't work out. I did the job throughout my pregency, until my maternity leave. There was a lot to the warehouse that Mrs. Tway did not allow me to do. She hired helpers for me. My helpers did all my lifting, drove the truck to the warehouse for supplies, and unloaded and loaded all the trucks. I remember one day, I had an empty box that I had picked up, Mrs Tway saw me with it and made me put it down. She was always very protective of the girls who were pregnant. But anyway, I handled the inventory for both shipping and warehouse. I also scheduled the packers shipping clerks who never worked out. During that time, we were moving into the new building, and I planned out

Figure 20, cont'd.

the warehouse in that building. As the ware was moved in I made sure it was put in the proper place. Then I went on maternity leave 2 weeks before I had my son, I came back 6 weeks later and got my shipping clerk job back, and I was happy. I worked in shipping for 4 years when I became pregnant again. I worked up until 2 months before my due date, and because of my health the doctor made me take my maternity leave in July. In September I quit because of baby sitter problems but returned to work 2 months after I had quit. The reason that I came back to Woodmere was because I loved it, the environment, people, everything. I did have an offer for another job, it was more money, but I wanted to go back home to Woodmere.

Decal Department. I returned to Woodmere and took over the decal department. I inspected decal, inventoried decal, and tested bad decal. I did that job about a year, but it was too boring. The Shipping Clerk and I traded jobs.

I worked in shipping 2 weeks and then took over the warehouse supervisor job. But this time around as Warehouse Supervisor, I'm not pregnant, know more about the company, and love my job. I do everything from mapping warehouses, scheduling deliveries, and pickups in the warehouse, to stacking skids of ware. I inventory ware, packing supplies, crystal, decorated dinnerware, and undecorated ware. I schedule the packers and shipper and supervise ware pulling for decorators, and keep both warehouses organized. At the present time I'm setting up the Recycling Program. I love what I do, and wouldn't trade it for anything.

I had worked for several different companies before coming to Woodmere 11 years ago. There were qualities that kept me with the company. Qualities that were not seen at any of the other companies that I had worked for in the past.

1) Everyone takes pride in their work, they are professionals.

2) Management is always open for new ideas, new ways of making a job easier, and more cost efficient. Bonuses are always given to employees that have a suggestion that

Figure 20, cont'd.

works, in making the job better. Because of the bonuses, employees always come forward with some really great ideas.

3) Everyone always has a fair chance for advancement with the company.

4) Anytime an employee has a problem with either a supervisor or a fellow employee, they always go to their supervisor, plant manager, or vice president. The problem would then get out in the open, get solved, and because of this it never would become a major problem. With all these women working together there have never been any cat fights in the studio.

5) We always have a calm environment,

6) It has alway been a clean place to work. We have professional cleaners come in daily to clean. All the employees are very clean.

7) We have a No-Smoking policy, and no one is permitted to smoke in the building. It pollutes the decals and gold. And also, it isn't fair to the employees who don't smoke to have to be surrounded with smoke. I'm a smoker and it doesn't bother me to go outside for a smoke.

We have never been successful with male employees. The problem that I have experienced with them is that they just don't care. They don't take pride in their work. All of the helpers that I have had have been male, and not one of them has ever cared. Wherever they put the skid is where they put it. They don't care if it's stacked correctly, or put in the right shelf. Personally I don't want to have to train another male for my helper again. It's just not worth it. I'm better off doing it myself, I always end up redoing what they did wrong. Then when you tell them they did it wrong, they get cocky and smart off. That's a problem you rarely have with women.

As far as anything I would have change about Woodmere, not a thing. If anything would have been changed it would not have been Woodmere.

LuAnn McAnallen Cassidy
5/6/91

Here is the executive secretary we hired from the temporary help agency I discussed in Chapter 2. You met her again in Chapter 5 when I discussed how to motivate employees and told you about her singing with the symphony chorus. In Chapter 7 I told you about our experiences teaching her to admit mistakes. She has a college education and proofread most of the letters our sales service people wrote. She also has a natural affinity for computers and was able to save us money by learning about computers on her own and sharing her knowledge with the rest of us. (See Figure 21.)

Figure 21
EXECUTIVE SECRETARY

On July 14, 1983, I began my career at Woodmere China. I was working as a temporary with Kelly Girl Services located in Youngstown, Ohio. My supervisor from Kelly Girls called me one morning and asked if I would be interested in taking an assignment located in New Castle, Pennsylvania. At first I was reluctant because of the distance from Sharon but I needed the work so I agreed to go.

I remember when I first tried to locate Woodmere. I got lost because I made a wrong turn on Route 224 and ended up in downtown New Castle. I called Woodmere and I finally found it even though I was late. My first day at Woodmere I typed some letters on the typewriter there, did some filing and learned how to get the in/out boxes. I started as Mr. Tway's secretary since the girl who was his secretary previously was no longer there. I was very nervous at first but the office manager, Linda Martin, made me feel at home.

The longer I worked there I enjoyed it more. In fact, I remember asking Bonny almost every day if she knew whether I was going to start there under the employment of Woodmere rather than Kelly Girls. I didn't know at the time if it was because I kept pestering her about this or if it was

Figure 21, cont'd.

because they were pleased with the quality of work I did (although I know now this is true) that I started under Woodmere's employment shortly after shutdown in January, 1984.

Mrs. Tway had several different secretaries when I was Mr. Tway's secretary. She always told me about the excellent secretary she had who got married and relocated with her husband to another state. I knew she really liked her and all of these new secretaries just did not do a good job. When the last secretary left, Mrs. Tway asked me if I would consider being her secretary as well as Mr. Tway's secretary. I was really scared at first because I did not know if I could do well in both of these positions. However, I was so excited to think that Mrs. Tway would want me to work with her that I said "Yes."

Working with both of them had its ups and downs when I first started. I know I made many errors but they were both so patient with me and were willing to work with me that finally I suceeded in doing a good job. But more than just learning how to run computers and all of the other secretarial duties, Mr. and Mrs. Tway taught me a lot of lessons that I now use in everyday living. They taught me how to be honest with myself, how to have self-confidence, and how to be assertive.

I always wanted to try my hand at being a customer service person and Mrs. Tway knew this. One time I was put into that position but the secretaries that were working in the office at the time were really novices. At the same time we just hired a new office manager as well. Although I wanted to work in this area, I was so nervous when I saw what was happening with the secretaries that I asked if I could please go back to being a secretary. Once again, Mrs. Tway allowed me to do what I wanted to do.

Shortly before they retired though, they knew I still had not given up my dream of being a customer service person, and they let me try my hand at this job once again. This time I succeeded in doing a good job and by this time,

Figure 21, cont'd.

Rose Saad had really matured in her secretarial skills, so being a customer service person worked out great.

If I were to change anything about my experience at Woodmere China I would only have changed two things. First of all, I would have been more open and honest when I made mistakes in the beginning. I know now that this was my major problem until Mrs. Tway showed me that by admitting my mistakes I would really grow in the company and not be looked down upon. The only other thing I would haved changed is that I could have been employed by this wonderful company earlier in my life so I could have had the chance to work with Mr. and Mrs. Tway longer.

Now I am going back to work on July 1 (after having had some time off for a maternity leave). I am looking forward to going back although Woodmere is not the same now as it once was because the Tways are retired and living in Florida. Woodmere China will never be the same since they are not here. They made Woodmere China a wonderful place to work and grow and I will never forget my early days working with them.

In Chapter 5 I discussed this young woman with several other key people who attended the symphony balls with us. Her loyalty and dedication are evident in her remarks. (See Figure 22.)

**Figure 22
BOOKKEEPER**

I started working for Woodmere China a week after graduating from high school, in June 1980. At that time the office staff consisted of Mr. Tway's secretary, Mrs. Tway's secretary, a bookkeeper, and myself, order clerk. My duties were taking orders over the telephone, manually typing them, and after shipping them, I typed the invoices to send to customers, and I did the filing.

At that time Woodmere had just purchased a computer system and the files were being set. Shortly after that the accounting department was moved upstairs along with Mr. Tway's office and secretary. I took over the position of computer operator. The bookkeeper was still there and they hired another girl to be the order clerk.

My first duties as computer operator consisted of working with the accounts payable and the general ledger. Later we put accounts receivable, sales order, inventory, and finally payroll on computer.

In July 1981 we moved into a brand new building we had just erected. Originally the accounting dept was downstairs with the rest of the office staff. Shortly there afterward they remodeled part of the upstairs warehouse into offices for the accounting dept.

Over the years Woodmere grew and grew, bringing the office staff to a count of 11 employees including Mr. & Mrs. Tway.

Everything I know about business I learned from on-site experience. They taught me everything, including how to operate computers. We now have several personal com-

Figure 22, cont'd.

puters for special reports and word processing besides the mainframe computer. Nearly every report generated at Woodmere is done on a computer. Most of our staff have computers right at their desks.

I have really enjoyed working for Woodmere. Everyone interacts with everyone else so well. The communication that goes on between employees is so tremendous. I have noticed when talking with some of our customers that their communication between departments is not very good. They never seem to know what each other is doing, or care to inform each other. We at Woodmere are always talking with each other and letting each other know what we are doing. I think that is one thing that has really helped Woodmere to become what they are today.

Karen Anderson

Here is the first vice president I developed to manage the plant and to take my job. She later got married, had a baby, and moved with her husband. When she left she was in her mid-twenties and had over $12,000 vested in our profit-sharing program. She had a high school education and had worked as a waitress before joining our company shortly after high school. She had already trained and developed her back-up before she got married. (See Figure 23.)

Figure 23
FIRST VICE PRESIDENT

I started at Woodmere China in May of 1979. I believe I started at slightly above minimum wage and was trained as an inspector of fired ware. If I remember correctly, the inspectors were, at that time, part of the packing/shipping department. For this reason, I was trained to be a packer as well. After a period of time, a supervisor approached me with an opportunity to learn to pen-line. She said if I did well, there might be an opening in the gold lining department. As it happened, I did well, and was trained further to be a gold liner. I loved that department and was a liner for about 1 1/2 years. At that time, there was an opening for someone to work in the kiln area. Since I had been working with liquid gold, and learned how to handle ware with extreme care, I was offered the change. The kiln department ended up to be my home for almost 2 years. I eventually trained as the kiln supervisor. Since I handled all the decorated ware, it soon came up that I had never trained as a decorator. That was quickly changed. I worked for several weeks until I mastered all the basic decorating techniques. Fortunately for me I learned quickly because after being so active on the kilns, I wasn't very fond of sitting all day to decorate. While supervising the kiln area, I learned to be a teacher and a trainer. I have always felt learning to operate, and in turn teaching to operate the kilns, was one of the most critical   and

Figure 23, cont'd.

responsible departments in the studio. Up to that point in production, each person was responsible for their own production. But once it got to the kilns, these people were responsible for everyone's efforts and could destroy anywhere from 1 to 800 plates in one mistake. I feel this is where I learned to be a conscientious worker. It was necessary and critical to pay close attention to details.

From there I was given the opportunity to assist the Plant Manager. While working as assistant, I was able to go into other departments I hadn't worked in previously, like warehouse/shipping, and be completely trained there. I acted as decorator and liner supervisor when needed, and rotated through all the departments as a "trouble shooter." I eventually became Plant Manager. I ran the decorating studio for about one year. From there I went into the office and learned our secretarial system, sales and accounting departments. Learning these departments, helped me coordinate the activities between accounting, the sales office, and the studio. In addition, the years of working and training in the studio helped me in my eventual position of Vice President.

When I worked there, one of Woodmere's outstanding features was the incredible opportunity they provided for a young person. Any employee at Woodmere could advance as far as they wanted to. They were always looking for good people who wanted to be promoted and take on any level of management. In addition, the person was compensated for their efforts. Each 2 week pay period, a person's pay rate was reviewed by their supervisor and Plant Manager to make sure they were being paid the correct amount. Another feature was the numerous incentive programs. Not only were there production incentives, but incentives for attendance, training, and even for good ideas. Bonuses were given to employees who offered an idea that was adopted to improve production. But above all, Woodmere made its employees feel important. From Plant Manager to the packer or warehouse person, each felt they were important in the "big picture." A lot of manufacturers make their end product the only thing that matters. At Woodmere, they made sure you saw the

Figure 23, cont'd.

results of your hard work and efforts and made you feel a part of the success of the company. Even when we won an industry award, it wasn't hung in the office, but in the studio, where the people who worked on the projects could enjoy it. Later, as a manager, I was very proud of how we treated our employees. No matter how busy we got, we never lost sight of who was responsible for the success, and treated every one fairly and with respect.

From a manager's standpoint, one of our most successful programs was cross-training. Employees were trained in several positions so they could be moved around as needed. I think this was a major contributing factor in the overall success of the company. Sometimes the nature of the business made production a little slow in one department and overloaded in another. We could move people to where they were needed to compensate for the difference in production levels and keep everyone working at a good pace. In turn, employees felt more productive and also proud of their accomplishments and ultimately happy in their work.

The work environment was busy and lively. This made everyone's daily duties not as routine, therefore not boring. We had contests and awarded weekly prizes. As a manager, we made a great effort to ensure the environment was a pleasant one. We spent a lot of time and money keeping the studio spotless inside and out. We wanted it to be a place people enjoyed working.

One of the things that was disappointing to us was our failure to successfully hire and develop young men. Since we were a decorating studio, we naturally attracted more female applicants. I personally think some of the young men who did apply, felt embarrassed to work with mostly females and thought the work seemed too feminine. Those who got past that had another problem. They didn't like being supervised by a woman. Then there were some who got past all of those things and showed interest in becoming part of our management team. Unfortunately very few succeeded. There were a variety of reasons for this ranging from immaturity to what we called "The Peter Pan Syndrome", but for the most part, I'll

Figure 23, cont'd.

focus on one. I personally feel young men fail to pay attention to details. At least ours had this problem. They usually skimmed the surface of a problem and picked up the highlights. Rarely did they go deeper into the problem to find out ALL the details in order to COMPLETELY solve the situation. This usually prevents the problem from reoccuring. We stressed this to our managers and made it a critical part of our managers' training. The worst part is they seemed too much in a hurry and couldn't even SEE the necessity of getting to the "root" of the problem. For this reason, they did not do well as managers, got frustrated, and a lot of times gave up.

Besides the special friendships developed by working at Woodmere, the career and travel opportunities I was given, and all the work and management experience I was gaining, there was one thing that kept me going. I loved the challenge! I always had something to work toward. I liked the fact you always knew where you stood and what was expected of you. This is critical in a person's performance. Although I'm sure there were things we could have improved upon, I can't think of anything at the moment that I would have changed. Being in management, anything we felt was wrong or could be changed or improved, was done at the time.

WORKING AT WOODMERE GAVE ME THE FOUNDATION I USE TO HANDLE EVERYDAY SITUATIONS IN MY LIFE. IT WILL STAY WITH ME ALWAYS....

Bonny Miller Eppinger

This young man represents one of our few successes with men. We had no more than two dozen such successes in the years we owned our business. He and those others represent the exception— not the rule of what we hired and lost or fired. He is the brother of our first vice president but did not join our firm until the year before we sold our business, long after his sister had left us. (See Figure 24.)

Figure 24
PRODUCTION SCHEDULER

I started at Woodmere in January of 1988. I was hired to become a supervisor, which requires training in all different departments. My first job was to learn how to decorate. This took about four days of practice. After that I went on to production decorating. I decorated for about three to four weeks. I didn't like decorating as much as most of the women that worked here did. Being a guy, I just didn't find it to my liking. Next I went to the lining department to learn how to hand line. It took about a week or so to learn how to do basic lines. It took a lot longer to learn how to do more advanced lining. I worked in the lining department for about two months. During this time I really grew to like this job. I didn't get advanced as I would like to have, but I had other training to do, and this was in the kiln department. Here, I think I learned the most (so far). I learned how to operate the kilns, how to load and unload, fire the decal or gold into a piece of ware and how to inspect the finished product. But there is more. I also learned how all the departments fit together. For example, a piece of ware gets decorated, it goes to the kiln and gets fired. It then goes to lining, where it gets gold lined, and back to the kiln to get fired again. Then it goes to final inspection.

It was really interesting to me to see how all the departments worked together to make a finished product. I enjoyed working in the kiln, not only because of how much

Figure 24, cont'd.

you see and learn, but also because of the mechanical aspect of the job working with the kilns. I worked in this department for about six months, then went on to the packing/shipping department. I learned how to make boxes for the different types and sizes of finished ware, then how to schedule different trucking companies, UPS, and Federal Express to pick up and deliver the finished product wherever it had to go. This job was also interesting to me, because it takes a lot of work to pack and ship ware, while making sure nothing is going to get broken during transport. Next I went to the warehouse and learned how inventory was kept on all incoming and outgoing shipments. Also, I pulled ware for the liners and decorators when it was needed. I then went upstairs to American decal. I didn't get too involved with the actual decal printing process, but did learn how to apply film to a screen. After more processing, the screen turns into a type of stencil. The screen is then used to push paint through it with a squeegee, onto a special paper. After more processing is done, the design you have created turns into a usable piece of decal. I also learned how to stretch a mesh fabric onto a square aluminum frame, which becomes the screen. I then returned to the kiln department, running the dayturn shift. I did this for about three months, then ran the afternoon shift for about six months, then onto running the midnight shift for awhile. All of the jobs listed, helped me a lot in preparing for the position of "Production Scheduling", which I have held for the past two years. I start by taking care of all samples that are done in the studio. I make sure they get decorated, fired, lined (if needed) and then fired again. I then make sure they get returned to the customer service person. I plan all production going through the different departments in the studio. I have to make sure all departments are doing what they are supposed to be doing and when they are supposed to do it, so as to meet committed ship dates. I also attend weekly production meetings with each customer service person to schedule ship dates on all new orders that come in. I am responsible for holding weekly shipping and quality meetings to go over all previous week's shipments and present week's

Figure 24, cont'd.

shipments and also to discuss any quality problems that have come up in the previous week. I am also responsible for holding all spec meetings to go over any special instructions on decorating, firing or lining a project. Last but not least, I attend weekly supervisor meetings where we all discuss any problems physical or mechanical, policies (old and new), and any new ideas that have been presented to us.

Overall I have found Woodmere China to be very rewarding in all aspects. I didn't work with Mr. and Mrs. Tway that long, but I feel that the way the company was handled and run from the beginning, was all for the good of the company and its employees.

Kevin Miller

RECOGNITION BY YOUR COMMUNITY

Recognition by your community is further proof of your success. The good things your employees say about you in the community contribute to your success. Word gets around that you are a good employer. Your good business dealings with service people in your community add to your success. If you have maintained high standards with them, they talk about it to others. Your good relationship with your local bank also proves your success.

When you start your business and as long as you are in business, you need money. Your relationship with the local bank is an important one. My husband, who ran the marketing and financial end of our business, always made a point of sharing as much information as he could with the vice president of our bank.

He never waited until we needed a loan before telling the bank all the good things that were happening to our company. He periodically put together brochures to show them. The brochures included the latest pictures of our product, notes about our newest customers, and news releases about our latest awards.

He purposely did it when we didn't need money. He wanted them to know who we were, how well we were doing, and how enthused we were about the business *before* we needed their help. He said if they know who we are and how we are doing they will remember us, and it will be easier to get money when we need it. He was right. (See Figure 25.)

If you can get the larger community to recognize your company, you can use it to sell your customers on the quality of your organization. We did that when we earned the coveted energy award during the energy crisis and used it to show our industry, our vendors, and our customers how well-run our manufacturing was. We showed how we passed this savings on to our customers. I talked about this in Chapter 8. (See Figure 26.)

PRESTIGE IN YOUR INDUSTRY

Prestige in your industry also proves your success. I mentioned in an earlier chapter that your success in your industry is important because it can affect your success with customers. When you receive industry awards, the free publicity contributes to your success. (See Figure 27.)

RESPECT FROM YOUR VENDORS

Respect from your vendors is proof of your success. How they feel about you is determined by the standards you set for them when they deal with you. If your standards are high, you will be successful with them. (See Figure 28.)

APPRECIATION FROM YOUR CUSTOMERS

Appreciation from your customers is the final proof of your success. You are in business to be successful with them. Success with them is what will keep you in business. I did not put them last because they are least important, but because everything else you do contributes to your ultimate goal—to please your customers. (See Figure 29.)

Designing and supplying our product for the president represents the ultimate proof of our success for us. (See Figure 30.)

Figure 25
BANK LETTER

APR 2 5 1985

FIRST NATIONAL BANK / OF WESTERN PENNSYLVANIA

101 EAST WASHINGTON STREET • P.O. BOX 1488 • NEW CASTLE, PA 16103-1488 • TELEPHONE: (412) 652-5511

THOMAS J. O'SHANE
SENIOR VICE PRESIDENT

April 24, 1985

Mr. Gene Tway
President
Woodmere China, Inc.
P. O. Box 5305
New Castle, PA 16103

Dear Gene:

I would like to thank you very much for taking time out of your busy schedule to share the Woodmere China Company with my colleagues and myself. Your organization is ever so impressive and both Patty's and your outstanding management abilities are evident throughout the company.

First National Bank appreciates and considers it an honor to be your bank, and I hope we can continue to provide you excellent financial services in the future. If I can ever be of service to you in the present or future, please do not hesitate to call upon me.

Very truly yours,

Tom

THOMAS J. O'SHANE
Chief Operating Officer

TJO/lmp

Figure 26
ENERGY AWARD

PENN POWER
The Energy Makers

1 East Washington Street
P. O. Box 891
New Castle, PA 16103-0891
412-652-5531

Pennsylvania Power Company

FOR IMMEDIATE RELEASE

Penn Power has recognized the owners of Woodmere China Inc. for their efforts to improve efficiency in their electric use. Woodmere received the "Load Management Award" and also the "Optimum Energy Award".

The Load Management Award recognizes successful results by customers in the use of electricity during Penn Power's "off-peak" hours. This gives the customers better control of their energy costs and allows the utility to make more efficient use of its generating facilities.

By controlling the demand of space heating and other electrical equipment such as kilns, Woodmere has achieved an annual operating cost savings of $11,900.

The "Optimum Energy Citation", received by Woodmere Inc., honors design excellence in overall thermal efficiency and use of energy-efficient equipment based on the actual amount of electricity used during a one-year period. Woodmere uses the energy from the kilns to heat the facility. Recipients of the award must meet or exceed Penn Power's minimum insulation standards for commercial building construction.

The awards recognition program was developed in 1979 by Penn Power's Commercial-Industrial Marketing Department to encourage the optimum use of electricity by its customers.

-022786-

Figure 27
INDUSTRY AWARD

RESTAURANT
HOSPITALITY

Scott M. Walters

Regional Marketing Manager

December 22, 1986

Mr. L. E. Tway
President
Woodmere China Inc.
PO Box 5305
New Castle, PA   16105

Dear Gene:

Congratulations on a fine showing in our November
Top-of-the-Table Awards issue.

Hope you enjoy this plaque.

Happy Holidays and much success in 1987.

Best regards,

Scott Walters
Regional Marketing Manager

SW/dmk

Enclosure

1111 Chester Avenue
Cleveland, OH 44114
(216) 696-7000
A **Penton/IPC** Publication

Figure 28
VENDOR LETTER

3310 N. Elston Avenue • Chicago, Illinois 60618 • Telephone 312/463-2122

February 18, 1986

Ms. Patricia Tway
Woodmere China, Inc.
Newcastle, PA 16105

Dear Pat:

Thank you very much for the hospitality you extended me last week during my visit.

I have not recovered from the overwhelming impressions that I received from your operation. You and Gene have created a remarkable organization and are justifiably deserving of recognition for such progressive management.

I have reviewed with Jean Zuckerman my visit, and, look forward to having another opportunity to discuss how we might work together.

Tell Gene I enjoyed meeting him and would be pleased for his input. During your April visit to Chicago, I would like you to join me for dinner. Please let me know if this is possible.

Cordially,

CHICAGO DECAL COMPANY

Calvin E. Nevin,
Director-Sales & Marketing

CEN:if

Encl.

P.S. You may find the two enclosed articles of interest.

Making Lasting Impressions Since 1932 • Representatives in principal cities.

Figure 29
CUSTOMER LETTER

UNICOVER
CORPORATION

One Unicover Center
Cheyenne, Wyoming 82008-0001 USA

Marketing and
Product Management
Department

Wednesday, December 11, 1985

Mr. Gene Tway
Woodmere China
P. O. Box 5305
Route 224
Newcastle, PA 16105

Dear Gene:

   We wish to express our heartfelt thanks at the effort that you have put forth in assuring that we will get our Statue of Liberty Plates in 1985. You have just proven to us, once again, that you are customer oriented and can be relied upon as a company that can solve problems creatively and effectively. Many thanks to you and your fine staff for your cooperation and help.

   This is to reiterate what was stated on the phone to John White on 12/10/85. You will be shipping out 1,700 plates on December 16, 1,500 plates by December 24, and 1,222 plates by December 27. It is understood that the December 27 shipment will be made UPS Second Day Delivery.

   Thanks again for a job well done, you literally saved our lives.

                              Kindest regards,

                              UNICOVER CORPORATION

                              Brian Hilt
                              Assistant Product Manager

BH:ce

Telephone: (307) 634-5911   Cable: Unicover Chey   Telex: 9109494079 Unicover Chey

Figure 30
PRESENTATION TO THE CARTERS

Pat and Gene Tway present the china custom designed for the Carters' fishing lodge to President and Mrs. Jimmy Carter.

Conclusions

In this book, you have the keys to provide a good workplace, but only if you use those keys collectively and consistently. Once you establish good management habits, you must keep them. The secret to keeping them is vigilance. Periodically take stock. Compare what you and your people did six months ago with what you do now. If any of you have been taking it easy and letting things go, you have begun to break your good management habits. Subtle changes discernible only to you now will be conspicuous to others later. They indicate an eroding of your standards. Never compromise your standards or you compromise your success.

The key to good management is common sense and consistency. The more predictable the environment, the fewer problems you will have with your people. To ensure this, you need to have good attendance and a good attitude, treat people as individuals, state your goals, establish policies and follow the rules, admit mistakes, teach, be open and flexible, take action now, probe deeper, discipline and document, plan ahead, follow through, communicate, and most of all care about your people. Remember:
- Hire people cautiously and selectively.
- Train people carefully and steadily.
- Motivate people creatively and individually.
- Supervise people consistently and assertively.
- Develop people conscientiously and carefully.

Epilogue

I began this book digressing about our own small business and how it grew from a mom and pop operation to a multimillion dollar enterprise. Since I told you we sold the business, I feel it's necessary to digress again before closing this book.

After fourteen years in the business, I didn't want to continue working full-time. If you own your own business, you work ten- and twelve-hour days. We did. We enjoyed it, and we were richly rewarded. But I wanted to move on. I had published a number of articles about our company and our industry in trade and consumer magazines. But it wasn't enough. I wanted to develop an advice column to help other small business owners. I started one two years before we sold our business. But I wanted to do more. I wanted to write books and teach about our experiences in business. I felt it could help others. I firmly believe that if you have acquired knowledge and experience in a field, you have an obligation to share it and pass it on to help others.

With those things as motivation, I decided to retire from the business, to shift gears and teach—by writing and speaking. Gene decided to shift gears too. We had worked together for so many years in so many different enterprises, he didn't want to work without me, and I didn't want to continue working full-time in our business.

As a typical entrepreneur, he can't sit idle. When he's not fishing or tying flies he's devoting his skills to handling our investments in the stock market. We're both busy. Anyone who starts a small business develops the habit of staying busy. You will discover this when you decide to leave your business.

How do you leave your business? You either pass it on to a relative or you sell it. We sold ours. Gene learned about investors who were interested in acquiring small companies, just like ours. They had more than enough money to take care of our employees and continue supporting the business the way we had.

When you sell your business, you have an obligation to find the right investor. You can never be sure how they will handle your business or your people, once you leave and they are in control. The best you can do is find people you think will carry on as you would, while knowing no one can do it quite as well as you can. Remember the chapter on letting go? It's hard to let go.

If you decide to sell your business, find the best, most respectable people you can to buy it. You can check their financial worth and their track record in business to make sure your people are safe and secure from a financial standpoint. Gene did a good job finding the right people with the right credentials to buy us.

What you can never be sure of, and never predict, is how they will manage the people you have hired, trained, supervised, and developed for your small business. You can only hope they will use the approach described in the preceding pages. Maybe they will read this book. I hope they do. I hope the people who take over your business someday will read it, too.

Index

FIND THIS BOOK HELPFUL?

Check these Useful, Informative Titles from Betterway

Homemade Money—Your Homebased Business Success Guide for the 90s, by Barbara Brabec. 328 pages, 8½x11, forms, illustrations, index. 1-55870-110-9, $18.95.

Cleaning Up for a Living, 2nd Edition—Everything You Need to Know to Become a Successful Building Service Contractor, by Don Aslett & Mark Browning. 208 pages, 8½x11, illustrations, forms, charts, index. 1-55870-206-7. $12.95.

Surviving the Start-Up Years in Your Own Business, by Joyce S. Marder. 160 pages, 6x9, forms, checklists, index. 1-55870-200-8. $7.95.

Small Businesses That Grow and Grow and Grow, 2nd Edition, by Patricia A. Woy. 264 pages, 6x9, index. 1-55870-126-5. $9.95.

Stay Home and Mind Your Own Business, by Jo Frohbieter-Mueller. 280 pages, 6x9, illustrations, appendices, index. 0-932620-83-3. $11.95.

Little People: Big Business—A Guide to Successful In-Home Day Care, by Gillis, Sawyer, Kealey, and Dempsey-Dubrow. 176 pages, 6x9, illustrations, index. 1-55870-212-1. $7.95.

Careers in Child Care, by Alma Lerner Visser and Patricia A. Woy. 176 pages, 6x9, forms, appendix, index. 1-55870-205-9. $7.95.

How to Make $100,000 a Year in Desktop Publishing, by Dr. Thomas A. Williams. 280 pages, 8½x11, photos, illustrations, forms, index. 1-55870-160-5. $18.95.

The Inventor's Handbook, 2nd Edition—How to Develop, Protect, and Market Your Invention, by Robert Park. 232 pages, 8½x11, photos, forms, appendices, index. 1-55870-149-4. $12.95.

GAMEPLAN—The Game Inventor's Handbook, by Stephen Peek. 136 pages, 8½x11, illustrations, index. 0-932620-85-X. $9.95.

Please try your favorite bookseller first. If all else fails, tell us what you want. Send the price of the book plus $2.50 for UPS shipping (for any number of books) to Betterway Publications, Inc., P.O. Box 219, Crozet, VA 22932.